2100 Powerful Sales Questions for Peak Performance

2100 Powerful Sales Questions for Peak Performance

Empower Your Salesforce with Targeted Questions to Transform Sales Conversations for Transformative Sales Results

Mindscape Artwork Publishing
Mauricio Vasquez
Toronto, Canada

Authors:
Mauricio Vasquez
First Printing: March 2022

ISBN-978-1-998402-19-9 (Paperback)
ISBN-978-1-998402-20-5 (Hardcover0
ISBN-978-1-998402-21-2 (Ebook)

INTRODUCTION

Questions are the cornerstone of discovery and understanding, both of which are essential in the dynamic world of sales. The ability to ask targeted, impactful questions is not just a skill but an art that can unlock doors to deeper insights, foster stronger connections, and drive sales success.

Why is mastering the art of questioning crucial in sales?

First and foremost, asking the right questions demonstrates a genuine interest in your clients' needs, goals, and challenges. It's a powerful way to show that you value and prioritize their success as much as your own. In the sales arena, your interactions with clients go beyond transactions; they are opportunities to build trust and create value. By engaging sincerely and seeking to understand your clients' unique situations, you lay the groundwork for fruitful, long-term partnerships.

Effective questioning enables you to align your solutions with your clients' objectives, addressing their specific requirements with precision. While you may have a broad understanding of what your clients seek, assumptions can lead to misalignment and missed opportunities. Insightful questions help you delve deeper, uncovering the real motivations and constraints your clients face.

However, the challenge often lies not in the act of asking but in crafting questions that elicit meaningful responses. Are your questions opening doors to new understandings, or are they merely scratching the surface? Are you truly listening to and leveraging the answers to drive actionable outcomes?

Reflect on this quote, which encapsulates the essence of effective questioning:

"The tough thing is figuring out what questions to ask, but once you do that, the rest is really easy." - Elon Musk.

Recognizing the power of questions is one thing; applying it strategically in sales to achieve tangible results is another. This is where this book comes into play.

You don't need to navigate the complexities of question-asking alone. I've distilled the essence of effective questioning into a resource that will transform your sales approach. This book presents 2100 powerful questions designed specifically for the sales context. These questions will not only help you uncover the insights needed to tailor your offerings, but also empower you to foster relationships that drive growth and success.

Embrace the questions within these pages as tools to sharpen your sales strategy, enhance client engagement, and ultimately, elevate your performance. With this book, you're equipped to ask the right questions that lead to meaningful answers—and those answers will be the key to unlocking your sales potential.

GUIDELINES FOR ASKING POWERFUL QUESTIONS

Mastering the art of questioning is crucial in sales, as it helps uncover the real needs and objectives of clients, fostering a relationship built on understanding and trust. Below, we provide tailored guidelines for asking powerful questions that can drive sales success.

- **Adaptability in Questioning:** Depending on the sales context, questions should be either open to explore possibilities or focused on gaining specific insights. Open-ended questions encourage broader thinking and discovery, essential for understanding client needs and challenges. Focused questions, on the other hand, help clarify details and make decisions.

- **Questions Aimed at Learning:** Your questions should aim to deepen your understanding of the client's situation, aspirations, and challenges. By stimulating thought and encouraging clients to consider new perspectives, you provide them with valuable insights and solutions that align with their goals.

- **Client-Centric Questions:** The primary purpose of your questions should be to benefit the client. Instead of seeking answers that merely serve your interests, focus on questions that stimulate the client's thinking, offering them new ways of considering their situation.

- **Engaging with Personal Responses:** Sales is not just about transactions; it's about relationships. Asking questions that invite personal responses creates a connection, showing that you value the client beyond the business opportunity. This engagement often leads to richer, more meaningful interactions and can be pivotal in closing sales.

- **Shifting Focus from Problem to Solution:** When clients are fixated on challenges, skillfully crafted questions can shift their focus towards solutions and future possibilities. This approach not only highlights your role as a problem solver but also opens avenues for collaboration and innovation.

- **Promoting Openness, Not Defensiveness:** The way questions are framed and delivered can significantly affect the response they elicit. To foster a conversation that encourages openness, questions should be non-judgmental and posed with genuine curiosity. Avoid starting with "why," which can make clients defensive; instead, use "how" or "what" to keep the dialogue constructive.

- **Facilitating Choice Without Manipulation:** The goal is to explore options together with the client, not to steer them toward a predetermined outcome. Questions should be open-ended to co-create solutions, allowing clients to arrive at decisions that they own and value.

- **Simplicity and Clarity:** In sales conversations, simplicity is key. Complex or multi-part questions can confuse clients or take the conversation off track. A concise, well-thought-out question can be much more effective in getting to the heart of what the client truly needs or believes.

By adhering to these guidelines, you can craft questions that not only improve client engagement and satisfaction but also enhance the sales process's effectiveness. Asking the right questions at the right time can be the key to unlocking sales success, building lasting client relationships, and achieving your business objectives.

TIPS FOR THE USE OF THIS BOOK IN SALES

In this book, we've curated a selection of powerful questions designed to enhance your sales process, deepen client relationships, and drive business growth. To maximize the value you derive from these questions, consider the following tips:

- **Organized for Reference:** The questions are organized into chapters based on different stages and aspects of the sales process. This organization is meant to serve as a guide; however, many questions are versatile and could be relevant to multiple contexts. Feel free to explore and apply questions across chapters as they align with your sales conversations.

- **The Power of Listening:** Effective sales conversations begin and end with listening. Pay close attention to your client's words, emotions, body language, and overall energy. This attentiveness will inform which questions will be most impactful and when to ask them.

- **Customization is Key:** While this book provides a foundational set of questions, the most effective use will come from tailoring these questions to the individual client and specific situation you're addressing. Personalizing questions makes your interactions more relevant and engaging.

- **Mix and Match for Depth:** Don't hesitate to combine questions from different sections or modify them to suit the flow of conversation. This flexibility can lead to richer insights and a more comprehensive understanding of your client's needs and challenges.

- **Space for Creativity:** You'll notice that some questions include variations and a blank option. This design encourages you to inject your creativity into the conversation, crafting unique questions that resonate with your specific sales scenarios.

- **Follow-Up for Clarity:** Leveraging follow-up questions is crucial for digging deeper into a client's responses. These questions can unveil underlying needs or concerns that may not be immediately apparent, allowing for more effective solutions.

- **One at a Time:** To maintain clarity and focus, ask one question at a time. This approach ensures that each question and its response receive the attention they deserve, without overwhelming or confusing the client.

- **Adapt to Your Voice:** While the questions provided serve as a template, adapting them to fit your natural speaking style will make your interactions more authentic and engaging. Your clients will appreciate the genuineness of your approach.

- **Continual Learning and Adaptation:** Use the responses and outcomes of these questions as learning opportunities. Reflect on which questions elicited the most informative responses and how you can adjust your questioning strategy to improve future sales conversations.

- **Flexibility Across Stages:** The sales process isn't always linear. Therefore, similar questions may recur in different chapters, reflecting their utility at various stages. Use them flexibly, tailored to the moment and your client's evolving needs.

- **Interchangeable Terms:** In this book, the terms "clients" and "prospects," as well as "products" and "services," are used interchangeably. Your choice of term should align with whether you're engaging with a potential or existing customer and whether you're offering a tangible product or a service.

- **Note on Question Similarity:** While every effort has been made to ensure variety, you may encounter questions that seem similar. This intentional design reflects the versatility of certain questions, which can be asked in multiple stages of the sales cycle. Embrace these as opportunities to refine your approach and understanding of each unique sales situation.

- **Types of Questions Based on Interaction:** The questions in this book are categorized to reflect different interactions within the sales process. Whether it's "*Salesperson to Client*" for direct client engagement, "*Client to Salesperson*" for anticipating client inquiries, "*Salesperson to Self*" for self-reflection, "*Salesperson to Colleagues/Internal Team*" for internal collaboration, or "*Salesperson to External Stakeholders or Partners*" for external partnerships, each category is tailored to optimize communication and facilitate a comprehensive understanding of various sales dynamics. This organization aids in preparing for a wide range of conversations, enhancing both the strategy behind and the execution of sales efforts. In this book, you will find 2100 questions classified as follows:

  - ➢ 600 questions - to be asked by "Salesperson to Client"
  - ➢ 600 questions - to be asked by "Client to Salesperson"
  - ➢ 300 questions - to be asked by "Salesperson to Self" (herself/himself)
  - ➢ 300 questions - to be asked by "Salesperson to Colleagues/Internal Team"
  - ➢ 300 questions - to be asked by "Salesperson to External Stakeholders or Partners"

HELP OTHERS EXCEL IN SALES

Your feedback and experience are valuable, especially to those looking to improve their sales skills. There are many sales professionals and individuals with sales duties searching for ways to enhance their performance. Your review could provide the guidance they need.

Think of your review not just as feedback, but as a recommendation and a sign of the book's value. If "2100 Sales Questions for Peak Performance" has given you useful insights or strategies, sharing your thoughts in a review could:

- Point others towards effective sales strategies and skills.
- Help someone improve their ability to mentor, lead, and close deals.
- Offer a new perspective or strategy that could be crucial for someone else.
- Encourage positive changes in someone's sales approach or career.

By leaving a review, you're helping to expand the knowledge and skills of the sales community. If you found this book beneficial, consider letting others know. The best tools are often those recommended by peers.

If you enjoyed the book, please leave a review where you bought it. Your input is very important.

To leave your review, please scan this QR code:

Thanks for your support and for promoting excellence in sales.

Best,

Mauricio

TABLE OF CONTENTS

1.   **RESEARCH AND PROSPECTING**

A.   **MARKET ANALYSIS:**

Understanding market dynamics is crucial for tailoring sales strategies and ensuring alignment with client needs and industry trends. The following questions serve as a guide for you, aiming to deepen market insight, identify opportunities, and refine strategies. They are valuable in the early stages of research and finding potential customers. They provide a systematic way to analyze market trends, competition, and customer behaviors. This makes decision-making and planning more informed and strategic.

(1) Salesperson to Client:

1. How do your current (strategies/objectives/_____) align with the evolving demographics of your target market?

2. What (challenges/opportunities/_____) have you identified within your market segment?

3. How have your customers' (needs/preferences/_____) changed in the last year?

4. In what ways do you segment your market to better address (consumer behaviors/purchasing patterns/_____)?

5. Can you share insights on how market trends have influenced your (product development/sales strategies/_____)?

6. How do you differentiate your offerings in a competitive market based on (customer feedback/competitor analysis/_____)?

7. What are the key (drivers/barriers/_____) affecting your market positioning?

8. How has your approach to targeting specific demographics developed to meet (market demands/consumer needs/_____)?

9. What (trends/technologies/_____) do you see as pivotal in shaping the future demand within your industry?

10. How do you use consumer insights to inform your (marketing strategies/product offerings/_____)?

(2) Client to Salesperson:

1. How does your solution cater to the specific (needs/challenges/_____) of our target demographic?

2. What evidence can you provide that shows your understanding of our (industry/market segment/_____)?

3. How do you stay ahead of (market trends/competitive shifts/_____) to ensure your offerings remain relevant?

4. Can you explain how your product/service can be segmented to address our varied (customer bases/purchasing behaviors/_____)?

5. What (strategies/methodologies/_____) do you employ to conduct competitor analysis?

6. How adaptable is your (product/service/_____) to meet the changing needs of our market?

7. In what ways have you used (customer feedback/market analysis/_____) to refine your offerings?

8. How can your insights into market trends help us achieve a competitive (edge/advantage/_____)?

9. What role does (customer behavior analysis/segmentation/_____) play in your sales strategy?

10. How do you plan to support us in targeting (new/emerging/_____) market segments?

(3) Salesperson to Self:

1. How well do I understand the (demographics/needs/_____) of our target market compared to our competitors?

2. What can I do to improve my knowledge of (market trends/consumer behaviors/_____)?

3. How effective are my current strategies at identifying and capitalizing on (emerging opportunities/market gaps/_____)?

4. In what areas of market analysis do I need further (education/training/_____) to better serve my clients?

5. How can I refine my approach to market segmentation to better align with (client objectives/sales goals/_____)?

(4) Salesperson to Colleagues/Internal Team:

1. How can we collaborate to enhance our understanding of (customer needs/market trends/_____)?

2. What resources do we have to deepen our competitor analysis and improve our (market positioning/strategy development/_____)?

3. Can we identify any (emerging trends/shifts in consumer behavior/_____) that may affect our sales approach?

4. How does our product development process incorporate insights from (market analysis/customer feedback/_____)?

5. What strategies can we implement to segment our target market and tailor our more effectively (products/services/_____)?

(5) Salesperson to External Stakeholders or Partners:

1. How can our partnership be leveraged to gain deeper insights into (market trends/consumer behaviors/_____)?

2. In what ways can you support our efforts to better understand the (needs/preferences/_____) of our target demographics?

3. Can you share how your expertise in (industry analysis/market segmentation/_____) has shaped your approach to the market?

4. How do you see our collaboration contributing to a stronger market (positioning/presence/_____)?

5. What (tools/resources/_____) do you offer can enhance our competitor analysis and market understanding?

B. LEAD GENERATION

Navigating the topic of lead generation requires a strategic approach to connect effectively with potential clients. These questions serve as a toolkit for you aiming to refine your strategies in attracting and engaging leads in diverse scenarios, such as engaging with clients, introspection, team collaboration, and partnership discussions. Use these questions to assess, adapt, and enhance your lead generation efforts, making sure they align with current market trends and customer needs.

(1) Salesperson to Client:

1. How can we better align our (content marketing/SEO strategies/_____) to meet your (information needs/search habits/_____)?

2. What (social media platforms/networking events/_____) do you find most valuable for discovering new (products/services/_____)?

3. How have you used (referrals/content marketing/_____) in the past to learn about (solutions/products/_____)?

4. In what ways can we improve our (online presence/lead tracking system/_____) to make our interactions more (efficient/effective/_____)?

5. What kind of (content/webinars/_____) would you find most useful in addressing your current challenges?

6. How often do you seek new (vendors/partners/_____) through (digital channels/trade shows/_____)?

7. What factors make you more likely to engage with a (company's content/social media post/_____)?

8. How do you typically discover new (products/services/_____) that address your needs?

9. Can you share an example where a (blog/eBook/_____) significantly influenced your decision-making process?

10. What improvements would you suggest for our (lead generation processes/customer engagement strategies/_____) based on your experience?

(2) Client to Salesperson:

1. How does your company tailor its (content marketing/SEO efforts/_____) to attract clients like us?

2. Can you explain how you track and organize (leads/prospects/_____) to ensure follow-up and engagement?

3. What role do (referrals/networking/_____) play in your overall lead generation strategy?

4. How has your online presence developed to meet the (changing needs/trends/_____) in our industry?

5. What success stories can you share about clients finding you through your (content marketing/SEO/_____) efforts?

6. How do you ensure the (relevance/accuracy/_____) of the content you produce for potential leads?

7. In what ways do you measure the effectiveness of your (social media campaigns/marketing strategies/_____)?

8. Can you provide examples of how feedback from clients like us has shaped your (lead generation strategies/customer service/_____)?

9. What strategies do you employ to keep your (internal records/social media profiles/_____) updated and engaging?

10. How do you differentiate your (lead generation/service/_____) approach to stand out in a (saturated/competitive/_____) market?

(3) Salesperson to Self:

1. Have I effectively used all available (channels/resources/_____) for generating quality leads?

2. How can I improve my approach to (identifying customers' needs/SEO/_____) to better attract our target audience?

3. What system adjustments are necessary to enhance the way I organize and track (leads/engagements/_____)?

4. In what areas do I need further development to better understand and leverage (current sales resources/social media/_____) for lead generation?

5. How can I more effectively measure the success of my (lead generation efforts/online presence/_____)?

(4) Salesperson to Colleagues/Internal Team:

1. How can we collaborate to enhance our (content strategy/SEO tactics/_____) for improved lead generation?

2. What insights have we gained from tracking leads that can inform our (marketing campaigns/product development/_____)?

3. Are there any (tools/technologies/_____) we're not using that could improve our lead organization and follow-up?

4. How can our (product development/marketing/_____) teams better support the lead generation process?

5. What feedback have we received about our (online presence/services/_____) that could help us attract more (leads/customers/_____)?

(5) Salesperson to External Stakeholders or Partners:

1. How can our partnership enhance our (lead generation strategies/content marketing efforts/_____)?

2. What (channels/platforms/_____) have you found most effective for generating leads in our target market?

3. Can you share insights or trends that might improve our approach to (lead generation/online engagement/_____)?

4. How do your services complement our lead generation goals, specifically in terms of (SEO optimization/content creation/_____)?

5. What collaborative opportunities exist for us to leverage our (networks/resources/_____) for mutual benefit in lead generation?

C.   LEAD QUALIFICATION:

These questions are designed to optimize the lead qualification process, a crucial step in identifying prospects most likely to convert. They help you assess a lead's compatibility with your offerings, decision-making power, and readiness to buy. You can ensure your efforts are concentrated on the most promising opportunities, improving efficiency and increasing the likelihood of successful outcomes by utilizing these targeted inquiries at the right moment.

(1) Salesperson to Client:

1. How do your current (budget/priorities/_____) align with the solutions we offer?

2. Can you describe your decision-making process and who has the (authority/influence/_____) in these decisions?

3. What specific (needs/challenges/_____) are you looking to address with our solutions?

4. How urgent is your need for a solution, and what is your ideal (timeframe/deadline/_____) for implementation?

5. How engaged have you been with our (content/brand/_____), such as website visits or content downloads?

6. In what ways can we better align our (sales/marketing efforts/_____) with your preferences for receiving information?

7. What has been your experience with our (lead generation/qualification process/_____) so far?

8. How do you typically assess the (value/ROI/_____) of solutions like ours?

9. What criteria are most important to you in the (evaluation/selection/_____) of vendors?

10. How can we facilitate a smoother transition from (interest to decision-making/evaluation to purchase/_____) for you?

(2) Client to Salesperson:

1. How do you determine if a prospect is a good fit for your (product/service/_____)?

2. What (information/resources/_____) do you provide to help prospects understand the benefits of your (product/service/_____)?

3. How do you prioritize customers, and where would our company fit within your (prioritization criteria/process/_____)?

4. Can you explain how you track engagement with your brand and the impact on lead qualification?

5. What makes your (sales process/lead qualification/_____) different from competitors in addressing our needs?

6. How flexible is your (pricing model/solution offering/_____) to fit within our budget constraints?

7. What steps do you take to ensure the alignment of your sales and marketing messages?

8. How do you address concerns or objections during the lead qualification phase?

9. Can you share success stories of clients with similar (needs/challenges/_____)?

10. What ongoing support do you offer post-purchase to ensure continued satisfaction?

(3) Salesperson to Self:

1. Have I effectively applied (Budget, Authority, Need, Timing criteria/other criteria/_____) to assess lead quality accurately?

2. How can I improve my ability to gauge a lead's engagement level with our (content/brand/_____)?

3. Am I effectively communicating the alignment between our solutions and the prospect's (needs/timeframe/budget/_____)?

4. How can I better prioritize leads to focus my efforts on those most likely to (convert/benefit/_____)?

5. What steps can I take to enhance the alignment between our (sales/marketing/_____) efforts for more efficient lead qualification?

(4) Salesperson to Colleagues/Internal Team:

1. How can we refine our lead qualification criteria to better match our target market's (needs/preferences/_____)?

2. What insights have we gained from tracking engagement that could improve our lead scoring model?

3. Are there opportunities to better integrate (sales/marketing/_____) data to streamline the lead qualification process?

4. How can product development contribute to enhancing the lead qualification process with insights on (customer feedback/usage patterns/_____)?

5. What adjustments can we make to our (CRM/cold calling/_____) system to better track and manage lead (engagement/progression/_____)?

(5) Salesperson to External Stakeholders or Partners:

1. How can our partnership strengthen the lead qualification process through shared (insights/resources/_____)?

2. What trends are you observing in lead behavior that could inform our qualification criteria?

3. Can you share best practices for aligning (sales/marketing/_____) efforts from your experience?

4. How have you successfully used (SEO/content marketing/_____) to attract high-quality leads?

5. What tools or platforms do you recommend for improving lead (tracking/engagement analysis/_____) in our industry?

D.   ADDITIONAL CONSIDERATIONS:

These questions are designed for you seeking to enhance the integration of technology into your sales process. Focusing on CRM capabilities and tech tools, they aim to uncover ways to improve customer service, streamline sales strategies, and ensure effective communication. Suitable for discussions with clients, self-evaluation, or team collaboration, these inquiries encourage reflection on leveraging technology to meet market demands and client expectations, ultimately enhancing the sales experience.

(1) Salesperson to Client:

1. How can our CRM capabilities enhance your experience with our (sales process/customer service/_____)?

2. What features do you look for in a (vendor's technology platform/CRM system/_____) that would make your decision-making process easier?

3. How important is (technology integration/automation/_____) in managing your interactions with suppliers like us?

4. In what ways can we use technology to provide you with more personalized (product recommendations/service offerings/_____)?

5. How do you see technology playing a role in improving our (communication/follow-up/_____) with you?

6. How could enhanced (data analytics/reporting capabilities/_____) from our (CRM system/customer service team/_____) provide more value in our communications and service to you?

7. What additional (automation tools/technology features/_____) would you find beneficial in receiving personalized updates or follow-ups from us?

8. In terms of technology, what are your expectations from us as a supplier to ensure a (seamless service/effective sales process/_____)?

9. How can we leverage our (lead management software/senior management/_____) to better meet your needs during (peak demand periods/specific campaigns/_____)?

10. Can you provide feedback on how our current use of technology affects your (decision-making process/purchasing experience/_____) with us?

(2) Client to Salesperson:

1. How does your company utilize (CRM systems/lead management software/_____) to promptly address my needs?

2. Can you show me how your technology platform can give me insights into (my purchasing history/service utilization/_____)?

3. What steps do you take to evaluate and update your (sales strategies/technology tools/_____) continuously, based on customer feedback?

4. How flexible is your technology in adapting to changes in (market trends/customer needs/_____)?

5. How does your lead qualification process benefit from your (CRM capabilities/technology use/_____)?

6. How does your company ensure that the technology used in the sales process adds value to us as (clients/end-users/_____)?

7. What measures are in place to ensure that data from your (CRM/lead management systems/_____) is used for continuously improving (customer service/sales strategies/_____)?

8.Can you explain how your technology platforms maintain my privacy and security while still providing personalized (service/offers/_____)?

9. How frequently does your team reassess its technology tools to ensure they are meeting the growing needs of (the market/your clients/_____)?

10. What role do I, as a client, play in shaping the (technology/tools/_____) you use for sales and customer relationship management?

(3) Salesperson to Self:

1. Am I effectively utilizing our CRM and lead management software to track and enhance my interactions with (clients/prospects/_____)?

2. How can I better leverage technology to automate repetitive tasks and focus more on (building relationships/closing sales/_____)?

3. In what areas can I improve my understanding of our technology tools to better serve (my clients/my sales process/_____)?

4. How regularly do I review and adjust my lead qualification criteria to stay aligned with (current market trends/customer feedback/_____)?

5. What steps can I take to ensure that our sales and marketing efforts are more aligned using (CRM systems/technology/_____)?

(4) Salesperson to Colleagues/Internal Team:

1. How can we work together to leverage our CRM system for more efficient (lead tracking/customer engagement/_____)?

2. What insights have we gained from our technology platforms that could inform our (sales strategies/marketing campaigns/_____)?

3. Are there any new (CRM features/technology tools/_____) we should consider to improve our lead qualification process?

4. How often should we meet to review and refine our lead qualification criteria to ensure they remain (relevant/effective/_____)?

5. Can we integrate any additional (technology solutions/data analytics tools/_____) to enhance our understanding of customer behavior and market trends?

(5) Salesperson to External Stakeholders or Partners:

1. How can our collaboration with you enhance our (CRM capabilities/lead management processes/_____) for better market adaptation?

2. What (technology tools/training/_____) do you offer that could help us streamline our lead qualification and (tracking/follow-up/_____) processes?

3. Can you provide insights or training on the latest (CRM technologies/marketing automation tools/_____) to improve our sales efficiency?

4. How often do you update your technology solutions, and how can we ensure we're using the latest (features/capabilities/_____)?

5. In what ways can we work together to ensure a seamless transition from lead generation to qualification through the use of (integrated technologies/shared platforms/_____)?

2.   UNDERSTANDING AND ADAPTING TO CUSTOMER BEHAVIOR

A.   CUSTOMER BEHAVIOR ANALYSIS:

Navigating the intricacies of customer behavior is pivotal for refining sales strategies. This collection of questions is tailored to dissect how digital interactions, peer influence, and personal values shape buying decisions. They're structured for conversations with clients, introspective analysis, collaborative team discussions, and engagements with external partners. Using these questions will enhance understanding of customer preferences, ensuring sales tactics are both responsive and anticipatory to market dynamics.

(1) Salesperson to Client:

1. How do your (purchasing decisions/social media interactions/_____) reflect the influence of digital channels?

2. Can you share how (peer reviews/social proof/_____) have affected your choice in our (products/services/_____)?

3. How do you perceive your own customer journey with our brand, especially through (digital touchpoints/physical interactions/_____)?

4. In what ways can we use (predictive analytics/customer feedback/_____) to anticipate your future needs more accurately?

5. How do (lifestyle choices/personal values/_____) influence your decision-making process when selecting a (product/service/_____)?

6. What (digital channels/platforms/_____) do you most frequently use to research potential purchases?

7. How important is (brand interaction/customer service/_____) in your overall customer journey?

8. Can you provide examples of how a personalized sales approach influenced your (purchase decision/brand loyalty/_____)?

9. How do you prefer companies to predict and respond to your future (buying behaviors/service needs/_____)?

10. What specific (customer experiences/brand interactions/_____) have significantly influenced your loyalty to a brand?

(2) Client to Salesperson:

1. How does your company analyze customer behavior to improve (product offerings/customer service/_____)?

2. Can you explain how customer feedback, especially through (digital channels/social media/_____), shapes your (sales strategies/business/_____)?

3. What measures do you take to understand the (psychographics/lifestyles/_____) of your target market?

4. How does your brand use (customer journey mapping/predictive analytics/_____) to enhance the purchasing experience?

5. How do you ensure that your sales approaches remain relevant in the face of changing (market trends/consumer behaviors/_____)?

6. What role does (social proof/peer reviews/_____) play in your (marketing/sales/_____) strategies?

7. How frequently do you update your understanding of customer (needs/preferences/_____) based on digital engagement?

8. In what ways have you adapted your sales process to better align with the digital-first (buying journey/customer preferences/_____)?

9. How does your CRM system track and respond to changes in my (engagement levels/purchasing behavior/_____)?

10. What strategies do you employ to keep your sales approaches aligned with current (consumer insights/market dynamics/_____)?

(3) Salesperson to Self:

1. How effectively am I incorporating (customer feedback/digital engagement data/_____) into my sales approach?

2. What can I do to better understand and anticipate my clients' (buying behaviors/future needs/_____) through predictive analytics?

3. Am I sufficiently considering (psychographic segmentation/customer journey mapping/_____) in tailoring my sales pitches?

4. How can I improve my use of (CRM technology/data analytics/_____) to enhance lead qualification and customer understanding?

5. What steps can I take to adapt my sales strategies continuously, reflecting changes in (market trends/customer behaviors/_____)?

(4) Salesperson to Colleagues/Internal Team:

1. How can we better integrate (predictive analytics/customer feedback/_____) into our (CRM/prospecting/_____) pipeline to refine our sales strategies?

2. What insights have we gained from (customer journey mapping/psychographic segmentation/_____) that can inform our product development?

3. How frequently are we revisiting our customer personas to ensure they reflect current (market trends/consumer behaviors/_____)?

4. In what ways can our sales and marketing teams collaborate more effectively to use (digital engagement data/social proof/_____) in targeting prospects?

5. Can we identify any gaps in our current understanding of the customer journey that might be addressed with (new technology/market research/_____)?

(5) Salesperson to External Stakeholders or Partners:

1. How can our partnership use your experience in (predictive analytics/customer behavior analysis/_____) to enhance our sales approaches?

2. What tools or platforms do you recommend for deeper insights into (psychographic segmentation/customer journey mapping/_____)?

3. How can we collaborate to ensure our sales and marketing efforts respond to current (consumer trends/digital behaviors/_____)?

4. Can you provide case studies or examples where your insights into (customer behavior/market trends/_____) significantly improved sales outcomes?

5. What emerging (technologies/trends/_____) should we be aware of to stay ahead in understanding and adapting to customer's behavior?

B.   PERSONALIZATION AND CUSTOMIZATION:

Personalization and customization are key to engaging today's savvy customers. These questions aim to guide you in tailoring your approach to match individual client preferences, enhancing the customer experience. By addressing these aspects, you can deepen customer relationships, improve satisfaction, and ultimately drive sales. Use these questions to assess and refine your strategies for delivering personalized and customized solutions that resonate with your clients' unique needs and preferences.

(1) Salesperson to Client:

1. How can we better tailor our (sales messages/product offerings/_____) to meet your specific (needs/preferences/_____)?

2. What kind of (dynamic content/personalized experiences/_____) would most effectively engage you and meet your expectations?

3. Can you provide examples of (personalization/customization/_____) that have significantly influenced your purchasing decisions?

4. How do you prefer to receive (product updates/sales communications/_____), and what customization would make these more relevant to you?

5. What (actions/behaviors/_____) should we monitor to improve our behavior-based segmentation and personalize our offerings?

6. How would you rate the effectiveness of our current (personalized marketing/engagement strategies/_____) in meeting your needs?

7. In what areas could we apply more (A/B testing/data analysis/_____) to refine our personalization strategies for you?

8. What specific (content formats/communication channels/_____) do you find most interesting for receiving personalized information?

9. How can we use your (interaction history/purchase patterns/_____) to better predict and fulfill your future needs?

10. What improvements would you suggest for our current approach to (dynamic content delivery/behavior-based segmentation/_____)?

(2) Client to Salesperson:

1. How does your company ensure that personalization doesn't compromise (my privacy/data security/_____)?

2. What measures are in place for (updating/optimizing/_____) your personalization strategies based on customer feedback?

3. How can I customize my (preferences/settings/_____) to receive more targeted (offers/communications/_____) from your company?

4. Can you show me how behavior-based segmentation influences the (offers/products/_____) I see from your brand?

5. What success stories can you share where personalized strategies significantly improved customer (satisfaction/engagement/_____)?

6. How frequently do you perform A/B testing to enhance personalization, and what impact does it have on customer experience?

7. How do you balance between automated personalization and human interaction in your (sales process/communication efforts/_____)?

8. What technology platforms do you use to achieve dynamic content delivery, and how do they benefit your clients?

9. How do you ensure that all personalized content is (relevant/up-to-date/_____) and reflects my current interests and needs?

10. What role do I play in shaping the personalization of your (sales/marketing/_____) efforts towards me?

(3) Salesperson to Self:

1. How effectively am I using (CRM data/customer feedback/_____) to personalize my sales approach for each client?

2. What can I do to improve my understanding and application of (dynamic content delivery/behavior-based segmentation/_____)?

3. Am I leveraging the full potential of A/B testing to refine my (personalization strategies/communication methods/_____)?

4. How can I better align my (sales messages/solutions/_____) with the unique preferences and behaviors of my clients?

5. What steps can I continuously take to evaluate and enhance the personalization of my sales approach based on (sales data/market changes/_____)?

(4) Salesperson to Colleagues/Internal Team:

1. How can we collaborate to enhance our use of technology for more effective (dynamic content delivery/personalized marketing/_____)?

2. What insights have we gained from A/B testing that could further refine our (personalization strategies/segmentation methods/_____)?

3. Are there new technologies or platforms we should consider to improve our (behavior-based segmentation/personalization efforts/_____)?

4. How can we ensure a seamless integration of (sales/marketing/_____) efforts to maintain consistency in our personalized customer communications?

5. What training or resources are available to help us better understand and implement (predictive analytics/customer journey mapping/_____)?

(5) Salesperson to External Stakeholders or Partners:

1. How can our partnership leverage your expertise or technology to enhance our (personalization efforts/segmentation strategies/_____)?

2. Can you provide insights or case studies on the effectiveness of behavior-based segmentation with similar (industries/clients/_____)?

3. What emerging trends or technologies should we be aware of to stay ahead in (dynamic content delivery/A/B testing/_____)?

4. How do your (products/services/_____) complement our goal of delivering personalized experiences to our customers?

5. What best practices can you share for integrating external data or insights into our (personalization/customization/_____) strategies?

C.   ADDITIONAL CONSIDERATIONS:

For you navigating the complex landscape of customer behavior, these questions are vital. They help refine strategies for feedback collection, personalization, ethical considerations, and technological integration. By exploring these areas, you can enhance customer experiences, respect privacy, and maintain consistency across channels. Use these questions to adapt your approach, ensuring it aligns with customer expectations and strengthens your sales process.

(1) Salesperson to Client:

1. How can we enhance our (feedback loops/customer service channels/_____) to better collect and act on your (suggestions/preferences/_____)?

2. What are your thoughts on (personalization/privacy concerns/_____) when interacting with our brand across different (channels/platforms/_____)?

3. How do you prefer to receive (personalized content/updates/_____), and what measures can we take to ensure it respects your (privacy/consent/_____)?

4. Can you share any experiences where (cross-channel inconsistency/over-personalization/_____) impacted your perception of a brand?

5. What (AI-driven recommendations/personalized experiences/_____) have you found most (useful/intrusive/_____) in the past?

6. How important is it for you that a brand maintains consistency in its messaging across all (digital/physical/_____) touchpoints?

7. In what ways can we leverage (AI/personal data/_____) to enhance your (shopping experience/customer journey/_____) without compromising your sense of (privacy/personal space/_____)?

8. How frequently do you prefer to provide feedback on your (customer experience/product satisfaction/_____), and through what (channels/methods/_____)?

9. What ethical considerations do you believe are most important when companies personalize their (sales/marketing/_____) efforts?

10. How can we better use your feedback to refine our (product offerings/sales messages/_____)?

(2) Client to Salesperson:

1. How do you ensure that the feedback I provide is used to improve your (products/services/_____)?

2. What steps does your company take to protect customer (data/privacy/_____) when personalizing marketing efforts?

3. How does your brand ensure consistency in (messaging/brand experience/_____) across all channels?

4. Can you explain how (AI/private data/_____) is used in your personalization strategies and what benefits it offers to (consumers/clients/_____) like me?

5. What mechanisms are in place for customers to (opt-out/control/_____) the level of personalization they receive from your company?

6. How do you balance between using (AI/public information/_____) for personalization and ensuring that communications remain (personal/relevant/_____)?

7. What policies does your company have regarding (ethical personalization/data usage/_____)?

8. How can I provide feedback about my preferences for receiving (personalized offers/communications/_____)?

9. How do you continuously collect and act on customer feedback to improve your (sales strategies/customer service/_____)?

10. What are the biggest challenges you face in maintaining cross-channel consistency, and how do you address them?

(3) Salesperson to Self:

1. How effectively am I using customer feedback to adjust my (sales approach/personalization strategies/_____)?

2. What steps can I take to ensure my personalization efforts are both (ethical/effective/_____) and respect customer privacy?

3. Am I ensuring consistency in my personalized messaging across all (digital/physical/_____) channels I manage?

4. How can I better leverage AI and machine learning tools to predict customer behavior without overstepping ethical boundaries?

5. In what areas do I need to improve to enhance (cross-channel consistency/customer experience/_____)?

(4) Salesperson to Colleagues/Internal Team:

1. How can we work together to establish more effective feedback loops that inform our (sales strategies/product development/_____)?

2. In what ways can we address ethical considerations in our personalization efforts to better respect customer (privacy/consent/_____)?

3. Are we maintaining consistency in our personalized messaging across all (marketing channels/customer touchpoints/_____), and where can we improve?

4. How can we better use (AI/predictive analytics/_____) to personalize our sales approach without compromising (customer trust/brand integrity/_____)?

5. What training or resources do we need to better understand and implement (ethical personalization/cross-channel consistency/_____)?

(5) Salesperson to External Stakeholders or Partners:

1. How can our partnership support the development of (ethical personalization strategies/advanced feedback mechanisms/_____)?

2. What insights can you provide on maintaining cross-channel consistency and the impact on (customer loyalty/brand perception/_____)?

3. Can you provide some recommendations on how to use (AI/CRM tools/_____) for personalization while respecting customer privacy and preferences?

4. How do you see the future of (AI/machine learning/_____) evolving to enhance (customer personalization/sales effectiveness/_____) while ensuring ethical considerations?

5. What tools or platforms do you recommend that could help us improve our (feedback collection/personalization efforts/_____) across all customer interactions?

3.   BUILDING RELATIONSHIPS

A.   ESTABLISHING RAPPORT:

These questions are crafted to assist you in the crucial stage of establishing rapport within the sales cycle. They are intended for use when starting contact with clients, aiming to personalize interactions and deepen connections. Through exploring topics like communication preferences, common interests, and effective listening strategies, these questions guide you in adapting your approach to resonate better with clients, laying the foundation for strong, lasting relationships.

(1) Salesperson to Client:

1. How can I adjust my (communication style/delivery method/_____) to better suit your preferences and ensure our discussions are as productive as possible?

2. In our conversations, what (topics/interests/_____) would you like us to explore to find common ground and strengthen our professional relationship?

3. Can you share how previous salespeople have successfully built a rapport with you, particularly through (active listening/empathetic responses/_____)?

4. How important is it for you that our interactions include (non-verbal cues/personalized communication/_____) to feel more engaged and understood?

5. What (hobbies/activities/_____) do you enjoy outside of work that might help us connect on a more personal level?

6. How do you prefer to receive information about (new products/updates/_____), and how can I make these communications more relevant to you?

7. What has been your experience with salespeople adapting their (pace of speech/language/_____) to match yours, and how did it impact your communication?

8. Can you provide feedback on how well you think I've been able to establish rapport with you so far, especially through (empathy/active listening/_____)?

9. What are some (non-business topics/interests/_____) that you're comfortable sharing, which could help us build a more personal connection?

10. How do you feel about salespeople using (personal anecdotes/humor/_____) in conversations to make the interaction more relatable and engaging?

(2) Client to Salesperson:

1. How do you ensure you're actively listening to and understanding my (needs/concerns/_____) during our conversations?

2. What strategies do you use to adapt your communication style to different clients, especially considering (cultural backgrounds/personal preferences/_____)?

3. Can you give examples of how you've used (empathy/small talk/_____) to build trust and rapport with clients in the past?

4. How do you balance professional boundaries with finding (common interests/personal connections/_____) to strengthen client relationships?

5. How do you maintain consistency in (engagement/communication/_____) across various channels (email, phone, in-person) to ensure a cohesive experience?

6. What role do you believe (non-verbal cues/body language/_____) play in building rapport during face-to-face meetings?

7. In what ways do you tailor your (sales pitches/presentations/_____) to match my specific interests and needs?

8. How do you handle situations where it's challenging to find common ground or (shared interests/rapport/_____) with a client?

9. Can you describe how you've leveraged (personal stories/hobbies/_____) to connect with clients on a personal level?

10. What importance do you place on (feedback loops/continuous engagement/_____) to ensure that our relationship remains strong over time?

(3) Salesperson to Self:

1. How effectively am I using (active listening/empathy/_____) to understand and connect with my clients on a deeper level?

2. What can I do to improve my ability to employ (non-verbal cues/adapting communication styles/_____) during client interactions?

3. In what areas can I seek common ground more proactively to enhance my rapport with (new/existing/_____) clients?

4. How can I ensure that my efforts to personalize communication don't cross into (over-personalization/intrusiveness/_____)?

5. What strategies can I develop to better adapt my (pitch/presentation/_____) to align with the unique preferences and behaviors of each client?

(4) Salesperson to Colleagues/Internal Team:

1. How can we as a team improve our collective ability to establish rapport with clients through (training sessions/workshops/_____) on (active listening/empathy/_____)?

2. In what ways can we share insights about client (preferences/interests/_____) to ensure consistent and personalized communication across the team?

3. What tools or resources could we leverage to better understand and adapt to the (communication styles/cultural backgrounds/_____) of our diverse client base?

4. How can we better document and share information about (client hobbies/personal interests/_____) to find common ground more easily?

5. What best practices should we establish to ensure that our communication across all channels remains (consistent/personalized/_____)?

(5) Salesperson to External Stakeholders or Partners:

1. How can our partnership help enhance the personalization and customization of our sales approaches to better meet client (expectations/needs/_____)?

2. Can you share examples of how your organization has successfully built rapport with clients through (technology/strategy/_____) adaptation?

3. What insights can you provide on effectively using (AI/machine learning/_____) to analyze client behavior and improve rapport-building strategies?

4. How do you ensure that your strategies for establishing rapport respect client (privacy/consent/_____) and maintain ethical standards?

5. What collaboration opportunities exist for us to leverage (cross-channel consistency/feedback loops/_____) to strengthen client relationships together?

B. EARNING TRUST:

Building trust with clients is crucial in sales, serving as the bedrock of lasting relationships. These questions, divided among key interactions—from salesperson to client, client to salesperson, and introspective queries—guide you on establishing credibility, understanding expectations, and showing reliability and transparency. Use them to foster trust, delve into clients' needs, and reflect on your approach to ensure integrity and commitment in every aspect of the sales process.

(1) Salesperson to Client:

1. How can we better demonstrate our (expertise/reliability/_____) through our communications and interactions with you?

2. What type of (testimonials/case studies/_____) would you find most compelling when considering our (products/services/_____)?

3. In what ways can we improve our follow-up on (promises/commitments/_____) to strengthen your trust in our brand?

4. How important is (transparency/honesty/_____) to you when discussing product capabilities and limitations?

5. Can you share feedback on how our current level of (communication/consistency/_____) meets your expectations for trustworthiness?

6. What actions can we take to ensure you feel fully informed about our (pricing models/service agreements/_____)?

7. How do you prefer to receive (updates/information/_____) that could affect your (decision-making process/business/_____)?

8. What measures can we implement to provide you with more transparent insights into our (product development/sales process/_____)?

9. How can we use (feedback loops/customer surveys/_____) to better align our strategies with your (needs/preferences/_____)?

10. What (values/principles/_____) do you believe are crucial for a salesperson to embody to earn and maintain your trust?

(2) Client to Salesperson:

1. How do you ensure that your expertise is up-to-date with the latest (industry trends/product innovations/_____)?

2. Can you provide examples of how your company has maintained (reliability/consistency/_____) in fulfilling commitments to clients?

3. What steps do you take to be transparent about (pricing/product limitations/_____)?

4. How do you handle situations where there's a gap between client expectations and product capabilities?

5. What protocols are in place for (following up/resolving issues/_____) promptly and effectively?

6. How do you personalize your communication to match my specific (needs/preferences/_____)?

7. Can you share a (testimonial/case study/_____) that shows how your solutions have benefited a client with similar needs to mine?

8. How does your company continuously improve your (services/products/_____) through the collection and action on customer feedback?

9. In what ways do you demonstrate (transparency/ethics/_____) when discussing potential challenges or limitations of your offerings?

10. How does your sales approach adapt to ensure consistency across all (communication channels/customer interactions/_____)?

(3) Salesperson to Self:

1. Am I consistently providing accurate and up-to-date information to my clients to uphold my (expertise/credibility/_____)?

2. How can I improve my follow-up process to ensure I'm meeting all my (promises/commitments/_____) to clients?

3. In what areas do I need to enhance my transparency, especially regarding (product limitations/pricing/_____)?

4. How effectively am I using (testimonials/case studies/_____) to build credibility with new prospects?

5. What steps can I take to better align my communication style with the preferences and expectations of my clients?

(4) Salesperson to Colleagues/Internal Team:

1. How can we collectively improve our knowledge sharing to ensure we're all equipped to show (expertise/authority/_____) in our field?

2. What strategies can we implement to ensure more consistent follow-up on our (promises/engagements/_____) with clients?

3. In what ways can we enhance the transparency of our (sales process/product information/_____) to build trust with clients?

4. How can we better leverage (testimonials/case studies/_____) across the team to reinforce our credibility in the market?

5. What measures should we take to ensure our communication is consistently reflecting the company's values and commitment to (transparency/ethics/_____)?

(5) Salesperson to External Stakeholders or Partners:

1. How can our partnership contribute to enhancing the (personalization/transparency/_____) of our sales approach to build trust with clients?

2. What insights can you share on maintaining (consistency/reliability/_____) in delivering on promises to clients?

3. Can you provide examples of how leveraging external (testimonials/expert endorsements/_____) has helped build client trust?

4. How do you ensure that your contributions to our sales process respect our commitment to (ethical practices/customer privacy/_____)?

5. In what ways can we collaborate to use (AI/other technologies/_____) to enhance (personalization/communication/_____) without compromising on transparency or trust?

C.   ADDITIONAL CONSIDERATIONS:

These curated questions are essential for you aiming to deepen client relationships through trust. Addressing personalization, professionalism, and problem-solving, they encourage a thorough evaluation of how sales strategies meet client needs. Ideal for various interactions within the sales cycle, these questions guide towards cultivating a trustworthy sales environment. Use them to refine your approach and foster meaningful, trust-based connections with clients.

(1) Salesperson to Client:

1. How can we further personalize our (communications/offers/_____) to better align with your (preferences/needs/_____)?

2. In what ways can I help solve your current (challenges/problems/_____) without immediate expectation of a sale?

3. What (professional behaviors/communication styles/_____) do you value most when interacting with a salesperson?

4. How do you perceive the impact of (social media presence/online reviews/_____) on your decision-making process?

5. Can you provide examples of personalized service you've received in the past that made a significant impact on your (trust/satisfaction/_____)?

6. How important is (punctuality/respecting boundaries/_____) to you in professional sales interactions?

7. What type of (content/information/_____) would you find most valuable for us to share with you regularly?

8. How can we better leverage (social proof/testimonials/_____) to reassure you of our credibility and reliability?

9. What are your expectations regarding follow-up and consistency in our (communications/service delivery/_____)?

10. How can we make our problem-solving approach more (visible/effective/_____) to you and your team?

(2) Client to Salesperson:

1. How do you ensure the information you provide is (personalized/relevant/_____) to my specific business context?

2. What strategies do you employ to maintain professionalism across all (interactions/communications/_____)?

3. Can you share how your company collects and acts on customer feedback to improve (service quality/personalization/_____)?

4. How does your company's (social media presence/online reviews/_____) influence your approach to building client relationships?

5. What measures are in place to ensure you're promptly following up on (commitments/queries/_____)?

6. How do you balance between personalization and respecting my (privacy/preferences/_____) in your sales process?

7. Can you provide examples of how you've adapted your communication style to better suit a client's preferences?

8. How does your company address challenges or issues that arise, demonstrating active problem-solving capabilities?

9. In what ways do you utilize (testimonials/case studies/_____) to establish trust with new clients?

10. How do you maintain (consistency/transparency/_____) in pricing and product capabilities discussions?

(3) Salesperson to Self:

1. Am I effectively personalizing my approach to address each client's unique (needs/preferences/_____)?

2. How can I enhance my active problem-solving skills to build stronger relationships, even when a sale isn't immediate?

3. In what ways can I improve my professionalism, including (punctuality/communication/_____), to earn more trust from clients?

4. How am I leveraging (social proof/online reviews/_____) to strengthen my credibility with prospects?

5. What steps can I take to ensure I'm consistently transparent and follow through on all my (promises/commitments/_____)?

(4) Salesperson to Colleagues/Internal Team:

1. How can we collaborate to ensure that our communications highly personalize and reflect attentiveness to client (needs/preferences/_____)?

2. What strategies can we share with the team to improve how we solve problems for clients?

3. In what ways can we collectively uphold the highest level of professionalism in all our client interactions?

4. How can we better use (social proof/customer testimonials/_____) across our (sales/marketing/_____) materials?

5. What mechanisms can we implement to gather and act upon customer feedback more efficiently to improve our (services/products/_____)?

(5) Salesperson to External Stakeholders or Partners:

1. How can our partnership help to create more personalized experiences for our clients through (technology/data analytics/_____)?

2. In what ways can you support our goal of active problem-solving for clients, possibly through (shared resources/expertise/_____)?

3. How can we leverage your (social media presence/industry reputation/_____) to enhance our credibility and trustworthiness with clients?

4. What strategies do you recommend for maintaining professionalism and punctuality in a fast-paced sales environment?

5. Can you provide insights or tools for better (collecting/using/_____) customer feedback to inform our personalization strategies?

4. TAILORING THE SALES APPROACH

A.   UNDERSTANDING CUSTOMER NEEDS:

To effectively tailor your sales approach, it's crucial to understand your clients' needs thoroughly. This set of questions is designed to guide you in probing deeper into your clients' preferences and challenges, ensuring strategies are closely aligned with client expectations. By addressing these questions to clients, self-reflecting, or discussing with colleagues and partners, you can enhance your approach to meet the nuanced demands of your clients, fostering stronger, more personalized relationships.

(1) Salesperson to Client:

1. How can we better personalize our (communications/offers/_____) to more closely align with your (preferences/needs/_____)?

2. What strategies do you prefer for solving your current (challenges/problems/_____) without immediate expectation of a sale?

3. What (professional behaviors/communication styles/_____) do you value most during our interactions?

4. How do you view the impact of (social media presence/online reviews/_____) on your decision-making process?

5. What examples of personalized service have made a significant impact on your (trust/satisfaction/_____) in the past?

6. How important is (punctuality/respecting boundaries/_____) to you in professional sales interactions?

7. What type of (content/information/_____) would you find most valuable for us to share with you regularly?

8. How can we better leverage (social proof/testimonials/_____) to reassure you of our credibility and reliability?

9. What are your expectations regarding follow-up and consistency in our (communications/service delivery/_____)?

10. How can we make our problem-solving approach more (visible/effective/_____) to you and your team?

(2) Client to Salesperson:

1. How do you ensure that the information you provide is (personalized/relevant/_____) to my specific business context?

2. What strategies do you employ to maintain professionalism across all (interactions/communications/_____)?

3. How do you collect and act on customer feedback to improve (service quality/personalization/_____)?

4. How does your company's (social media presence/online reviews/_____) influence your approach to building client relationships?

5. What measures are in place to ensure you're promptly following up on (commitments/queries/_____)?

6. How do you balance between personalization and respecting my (privacy/preferences/_____) in your sales process?

7. Can you provide examples of how you've adapted your communication style to better suit a client's preferences?

8. How do you address challenges or issues that arise, demonstrating active problem-solving capabilities?

9. In what ways do you utilize (testimonials/case studies/_____) to establish trust with new clients?

10. How do you maintain (consistency/transparency/_____) in pricing and product capabilities discussions?

(3) Salesperson to Self:

1. How effectively am I using (open-ended questions/active listening/_____) to uncover my clients' (true needs/motivations/_____)?

2. What strategies can I develop to better address the (emotional drivers/underlying motivations/_____) behind my clients' purchasing decisions?

3. Am I consistently (summarizing/reflecting back/_____) what I've heard to confirm my understanding of (clients' needs/expectations/_____)?

4. How can I enhance my approach to (layered questioning/personalized communication/_____) to delve deeper into (clients' stated needs/underlying challenges/_____)?

5. In what ways can I improve my use of (customer feedback/interaction history/_____) to personalize my (communication/proposals/_____) more effectively?

(4) Salesperson to Colleagues/Internal Team:

1. How can we collaborate to refine our (needs analysis process/client engagement strategies/_____) to ensure they are (comprehensive/client-focused/_____)?

2. What (training/resources/_____) are available that could improve our skills in (identifying emotional drivers/customizing our communication/_____)?

3. Can we establish a process for sharing (best practices/successful case studies/_____) where a deep understanding of customer needs led to (successful sales/enhanced relationships/_____)?

4. How can we better leverage (technology/tools/_____) to track and analyze (client interactions/feedback/_____) for deeper insights into their needs?

5. What mechanisms should we put in place to ensure that our communication is consistently (personalized/aligned with client preferences/_____) across all touchpoints?

(5) Salesperson to External Stakeholders or Partners:

1. In what ways can our partnership enhance our ability to (understand/meet/_____) the complex needs of our clients through (additional insights/technology support/_____)?

2. Can you share (insights/data/_____) that could help us tailor our sales approach to better meet the (evolving needs/preferences/_____) of our market?

3. How can your (products/services/_____) complement ours to provide a more (holistic/complete/_____) solution to our clients?

4. What have you learned from your experience in needs analysis and understanding emotional drivers that could help us (improve our sales approach/enhance client relationships/_____)?

5. Which (tools/platforms/_____) do you recommend for conducting a thorough needs analysis and tracking (client preferences/engagement/_____) over time?

B.   PRESENTATION OF SOLUTION:

This set of questions is designed to help you tailor your solution presentations to the unique needs and preferences of your clients. Focusing on personalized demonstrations, storytelling, and addressing specific challenges, these questions guide you in making your solutions more relevant and compelling. By refining how solutions are presented, you can better align with client expectations, demonstrate value, and significantly improve the chances of winning over potential clients.

(1) Salesperson to Client:

1. How can we tailor our (product demonstrations/service examples/_____) to directly address your (specific needs/challenges/_____)?

2. In what ways can storytelling about our (products/services/_____) help illustrate the benefits for your particular situation?

3. What aspects of our (product/service/_____) do you find most compelling when compared to (competitors/other solutions/_____)?

4. Can you provide feedback on how our proposed solution aligns with your (expectations/pain points/_____)?

5. How important is it for you to see (customized demonstrations/personalized examples/_____) of our product in action?

6. What specific (features/attributes/_____) of our product do you believe could best solve your current challenges?

7. How do you prefer to receive information about our product's (unique value/competitive advantages/_____)?

8. Can we discuss a time when a (product/service/_____) fell short of meeting your needs and how you wish the situation was handled?

9. What (emotional drivers/motivations/_____) influence your decision-making process the most when considering new products?

10. How can we improve our presentation to make our (solutions/benefits/_____) more relatable to your business context?

(2) Client to Salesperson:

1. How do you ensure your product's features are directly relevant to my (business needs/specific challenges/_____)?

2. What makes your (product/service/_____) stand out from competitors in terms of addressing my unique needs?

3. Can you share stories of how your product has solved problems for other clients with similar (challenges/requirements/_____)?

4. How do you customize your product demonstrations to reflect the potential impact on my (operations/business/_____)?

5. What steps do you take to fully understand my (business's needs/personal needs/_____) before presenting your solution?

6. How transparent are you about your product's (limitations/pricing/_____) during the sales process?

7. What kind of follow-up can I expect after a product demonstration or presentation?

8. How does your value proposition align with the (long-term goals/strategic objectives/_____) of my business?

9. In what ways do you use (customer feedback/industry trends/_____) to continuously improve your product presentations?

10. How do you incorporate (emotional drivers/personalized storytelling/_____) into your sales approach to make the solution more appealing?

(3) Salesperson to Self:

1. How effectively am I aligning our (product/service/_____) features with the customer's specific (needs/pain points/_____) in my presentations?

2. In what ways can I improve my storytelling skills to highlight the real-world applications and benefits of our solution?

3. Am I providing (customized demonstrations/personalized examples/_____) that clearly relate to each customer's unique situation?

4. How clearly am I articulating our value proposition and its distinction from (competitors/other solutions/_____)?

5. What additional steps can I take to ensure that I fully tailor my sales approach to address the (emotional/strategic/_____) drivers of my clients' decisions?

(4) Salesperson to Colleagues/Internal Team:

1. How can we collaborate to enhance the customization of our (demonstrations/product presentations/_____) for potential clients?

2. What strategies have you found effective in incorporating storytelling into our sales presentations to illustrate benefits more vividly?

3. Can we share (insights/feedback/_____) to refine our value proposition, making it more convincing to our target (audience/market/_____)?

4. What action plans can we establish for identifying and addressing the emotional drivers behind customers' purchasing decisions?

5. How can we ensure consistency in conveying our product's unique value across all client (interactions/presentations/_____)?

(5) Salesperson to External Stakeholders or Partners:

1. How can our partnership enhance the personalization and effectiveness of our (product demonstrations/sales presentations/_____)?

2. Can you provide examples or case studies where your (insights/technology/_____) improved the presentation of solutions to clients?

3. In what ways can your expertise help us better understand and articulate the unique value proposition of our solutions to customers?

4. How do you suggest we leverage (social proof/external validation/_____) to strengthen the credibility of our presentations?

5. What (tools/resources/_____) do you offer that could help us create more engaging and tailored sales presentations for our diverse client base?

C.   ADDITIONAL CONSIDERATIONS:

These questions guide you in tailoring your approach to align closely with client needs and feedback. They emphasize the importance of customizing presentations and demonstrations, effectively handling objections, and using visual aids and testimonials to illustrate the solution's benefits. This strategic approach aims to enhance client engagement, build trust, and facilitate informed decision-making, ensuring that the sales presentation resonates with the client's specific challenges and goals.

(1) Salesperson to Client:

1. How can we adapt our (presentation/demonstration/_____) based on your (feedback/questions/_____) to better meet your needs?

2. Which (benefits/features/_____) of our solution do you find most relevant to your (current challenges/goals/_____)?

3. In what ways can (visual aids/testimonials/_____) help clarify the benefits of our solution for you?

4. How do you prefer we address any (initial objections/concerns/_____) you might have during our presentation?

5. Can you share how previous sales presentations have (met/fallen short of/_____) your expectations in terms of (flexibility/responsiveness/_____)?

6. What format of (visual aids/supporting materials/_____) do you find most engaging and informative?

7. How important is it for you we prioritize addressing your most (pressing needs/immediate challenges/_____) early in our presentation?

8. Could you provide examples of how a customized demonstration has influenced your decision-making process in the past?

9. What specific (objections/questions/_____) do you expect having about our (solution/product/_____), and how can we prepare to address them effectively?

10. How can we better use (customer testimonials/real-world examples/_____) to enhance the credibility of our (presentation/value/_____)?

(2) Client to Salesperson:

1. How do you ensure your (presentations/services/_____) are (tailored/personalized/_____) to each client's unique (needs/situation/_____)?

2. What strategies do you use to adapt your (presentation/products/_____) in real-time based on (audience feedback/client questions/_____)?

3. How do you decide which benefits of your solution to prioritize when presenting to a potential client like me?

4. Can you provide examples of how you've used (visual aids/testimonials/_____) to support your points effectively in the past?

5. How do you typically handle (objections/criticisms/_____) during your sales presentations?

6. In what ways do you customize demonstrations to highlight how your (solution/post sales support/_____) addresses my specific (challenges/requirements/_____)?

7. How transparent are you about addressing potential limitations of your product during your presentations?

8. What steps do you take to clearly communicate and ensure understanding of the value your (solution/company/_____) offers?

9. How do you incorporate feedback received during presentations into future (sales strategies/product development/_____)?

10. What role do (visual aids/supporting documents/_____) play in your presentations, and how do they enhance understanding?

(3) Salesperson to Self:

1. How effectively am I incorporating (real-time feedback/adapting strategies/_____) into my presentations to enhance client engagement?

2. Am I effectively (prioritizing/communicating/_____) the benefits most relevant to each client's (specific needs/challenges/_____)?

3. How can I improve my use of (visual aids/supporting materials/_____) to make my presentations more compelling and understandable?

4. Am I adequately prepared to address and integrate (initial objections/client concerns/_____) into my presentation seamlessly?

5. What additional steps can I take to ensure that I fully tailor my sales approach to address the (emotional/strategic/_____) drivers of my clients' decisions?

(4) Salesperson to Colleagues/Internal Team:

1. How can we collaborate to ensure that we adjust our sales presentations dynamically based on (client feedback/observed reactions/_____)?

2. What best practices can we share for effectively prioritizing and presenting the benefits that matter most to our clients?

3. How can we enhance our use of (visual aids/testimonials/_____) to support our presentations and make our solution's benefits more tangible?

4. What strategies have we found effective for (anticipating/addressing/_____) common objections during our presentations?

5. How can we make better use of our team's (knowledge/experiences/_____) to enhance how we communicate the value of our solution?

(5) Salesperson to External Stakeholders or Partners:

1. How can our collaboration help enhance the (personalization/adaptability/_____) of our sales presentations to address client feedback more effectively?

2. In what ways can your (expertise/resources/_____) assist us in creating more impactful (visual aids/supporting materials/_____) for our presentations?

3. Can you share (insights/tactics/_____) that could help us better anticipate and prepare for initial objections during our sales presentations?

4. How do your (solutions/services/_____) enable us to more effectively communicate our product's value proposition to potential clients?

5. What feedback or data do you provide that could help us prioritize benefits more accurately according to each client's specific (needs/interests/_____)?

5. CRAFTING COMPELLING SALES NARRATIVES

A.   IDENTIFYING THE CORE NARRATIVE:

Developing a compelling sales narrative is essential for connecting with clients and showcasing your offering's value. These questions guide you in creating narratives that resonate with clients' needs and challenges. They focus on aligning the offering's story with customer values and addressing specific pain points through feedback, case studies, and real-world examples. This approach aims to enhance client engagement and facilitate decision-making by making the narrative relevant and persuasive.

(1) Salesperson to Client:

1. How can I develop a (story/narrative/_____) that resonates with your (needs/challenges/_____) and highlights our solution's unique value?

2. What specific (problems/needs/_____) do you face that our product could address in its core narrative?

3. Can you share an experience where a product's (story/value proposition/_____) made a significant impact on your decision-making process?

4. How important is it for you that our product's narrative clearly outlines how it (solves specific problems/fulfills specific needs/_____)?

5. What elements of a sales narrative do you find most compelling when considering new (products/services/_____)?

6. In what ways can we incorporate your (feedback/experiences/_____) into our product's central story?

7. How can our narrative better demonstrate the (benefits/impact/_____) of our solution on your business operations?

8. What (aspects/values/_____) of your company's mission should our narrative align with to resonate more effectively?

9. Can you provide examples of (challenges/pain points/_____) that should be addressed directly in our narrative?

10. How do you prefer to see our product's (features/benefits/_____) presented within the narrative to ensure clarity and engagement?

(2) Client to Salesperson:

1. How do you tailor your product's narrative to address my specific (industry/business/_____) needs?

2. Can you explain how your product's story aligns with our company's (values/goals/_____)?

3. What makes your product's narrative different from (competitors/other offerings/_____) in the market?

4. How do you ensure the narrative is (relevant/compelling/_____) to decision-makers like myself?

5. How is feedback from clients like us incorporated into developing your product's (story/narrative/_____)?

6. What (evidence/testimonials/_____) do you use to support the claims made in your (service's/product's/_____) narrative?

7. How do you adapt the narrative when faced with initial (objections/skepticism/_____) from potential clients?

8. Can you provide a case study where your narrative significantly influenced a client's (decision/purchase/_____)?

9. How does your narrative address common (misconceptions/doubts/_____) about your (product/service/_____)?

10. What role do (visual aids/demonstrations/_____) play in enhancing your product's narrative during presentations?

(3) Salesperson to Self:

1. How effectively am I developing and communicating a core narrative that (resonates with/connects to/_____) my clients' needs?

2. What aspects of our product's narrative could be improved to more clearly highlight its (unique value/benefits/_____)?

3. How can I better use (customer feedback/success stories/_____) to refine our narrative and make it more compelling?

4. In what ways can I ensure that our narrative remains (flexible/adaptable/_____) to address various customer scenarios?

5. What steps can I take to deepen my understanding of clients' needs to craft narratives that is (engaging/relevant/_____)?

(4) Salesperson to Colleagues/Internal Team:

1. How can we collaborate to strengthen our product's core narrative by incorporating (diverse perspectives/real-world examples/_____)?

2. What (best practices/tactics/_____) have we identified for crafting narratives that effectively communicate the product's (value/impact/_____)?

3. How can we better integrate (customer testimonials/feedback/_____) into our narrative to enhance credibility and relatability?

4. What strategies can we employ to ensure our narrative addresses and prioritizes clients' most pressing (needs/challenges/_____)?

5. In what ways can we leverage (visual aids/supporting materials/_____) to make our narrative more tangible and convincing to clients?

(5) Salesperson to External Stakeholders or Partners:

1. How can our partnership enrich the narrative we're developing by highlighting (synergies/additional benefits/_____)?

2. Can you provide (insights/data/_____) that could help us make our narrative more (relevant/impactful/_____) to our target audience?

3. In what ways can your (expertise/resources/_____) help us address common objections within our narrative more (effectively/convincingly/_____)?

4. How do you suggest we incorporate (market trends/consumer behavior insights/_____) into our narrative to ensure it remains current and compelling?

5. What role can (third-party endorsements/collaborative case studies/_____) play in strengthening the credibility of our narrative in the eyes of potential clients?

B.   CHARACTER AND CONFLICT:

Crafting compelling sales narratives involves positioning the client as the hero of a story where your product or service aids in overcoming challenges. This set of questions is designed to help you tailor their narratives to highlight the unique value of their solutions, align with the client's goals and challenges, and illustrate the transformative impact on the client's journey. Effective storytelling in sales makes the value proposition more relatable and persuasive, enhancing client engagement and decision-making.

(1) Salesperson to Client:

1. How can we best portray you as the (hero/champion/_____) in our narrative, overcoming (challenges/obstacles/_____) with our (product/service/_____) as your ally?

2. What are the primary (challenges/goals/_____) your organization is looking to overcome, and how can our solution play a role in that journey?

3. Can you share a story where you successfully overcame a (challenge/obstacle/_____) that might reflect the journey we're proposing with our solution?

4. How do you envision our (product/service/_____) fitting into your story of (growth/transformation/_____)?

5. What attributes of a (product/service/_____) make it the ideal ally for you in achieving your (goals/objectives/_____)?

6. How important is it for the narrative to include real-world examples of similar (heroes/organizations/_____) overcoming their challenges with our help?

7. In what ways can we customize our story to reflect the unique (culture/values/_____) of your organization?

8. Can you describe past experiences where a product's role in your story significantly influenced your decision to (purchase/partner/_____)?

9. What kind of (conflicts/challenges/_____) do you foresee in achieving your goals, and how can our solution help address these?

10. How can our narrative help illuminate the path to overcoming your current (barriers/limitations/_____) with our (product/service/_____)?

(2) Client to Salesperson:

1. How does your product's narrative align with our company's mission of (overcoming challenges/achieving goals/_____)?

2. Can you demonstrate how others in my position have been the hero of their story by partnering with your (product/service/_____)?

3. What makes your (product/service/_____) the right ally for my company in our current (challenge/situation/_____)?

4. How do you tailor your narratives to different industries or companies with unique (challenges/cultures/_____)?

5. How flexible is your narrative approach when faced with a client who has unconventional (needs/goals/_____)?

6. How can your (product/service/_____) act as a catalyst in our company's story of (transformation/growth/_____)?

7. What examples can you provide where your solution has been a key ally in helping businesses overcome similar (obstacles/challenges/_____) to ours?

8. How do you ensure that your narrative doesn't just sell a product but genuinely contributes to our story of (success/innovation/_____)?

9. Can you illustrate how your (service/product/_____) has evolved to meet the changing needs of your clients, becoming an integral part of their success stories?

10. In what ways do you gather and utilize (customer feedback/stories/_____) to continually refine and personalize your sales narrative to new prospects?

(3) Salesperson to Self:

1. Am I effectively positioning my clients as the (hero/main character/_____) in the narratives I create around our (product/service/_____)?

2. How can I better identify and articulate the (conflicts/challenges/_____) my clients face that our solution can help resolve?

3. What steps can I take to ensure my narratives are (engaging/relevant/_____) to the specific needs and goals of each client?

4. How can I improve my ability to adapt the narrative based on (real-time feedback/client input/_____)?

5. In what ways can I enhance the storytelling aspect of my sales approach to make the (value/benefits/_____) of our solution more tangible?

(4) Salesperson to Colleagues/Internal Team:

1. How can we work together to craft narratives that effectively position our clients as the (hero/protagonist/_____) in their journey with our (product/service/_____)?

2. What resources or (training/sessions/_____) can we provide to our team to improve our ability to identify and articulate client (conflicts/challenges/_____)?

3. Can we share (success stories/case studies/_____) where our narrative approach has significantly impacted a client's decision-making process?

4. How can we ensure our narratives consistently reflect the unique (values/missions/_____) of our clients and their industries?

5. What feedback mechanisms can we implement to gather insights on the effectiveness of our narratives from both clients and (prospects/stakeholders/_____)?

(5) Salesperson to External Stakeholders or Partners:

1. In what ways can our partnership enhance the narratives we create, providing (tools/resources/_____) that further empower our clients as the heroes of their stories?

2. Can you share insights or data on (industry trends/client challenges/_____) that can help us refine our storytelling approach?

3. How can we leverage your (expertise/products/_____) to address the conflicts and challenges our clients face more effectively in our narratives?

4. What role can (third-party endorsements/collaborative efforts/_____) play in strengthening the credibility of our narratives in the eyes of potential clients?

5. How do you suggest we adapt our narratives to stay (relevant/compelling/_____) in a rapidly changing (market/industry/_____)?

C.   EMOTIONAL ENGAGEMENT:

These questions guide you in creating narratives that resonate emotionally with clients, emphasizing the importance of aligning with your values and challenges. You are encouraged to explore how products or services can become part of the client's success story, ensuring they personalize and make their narratives emotionally compelling. This approach aims to deepen client relationships, making the sales narrative not just a pitch, but a story of mutual growth and understanding.

(1) Salesperson to Client:

1. How can we better connect our narrative to the (emotions/values/_____) that matter most to your (team/organization/_____)?

2. What stories from your company can we integrate that deeply resonate with your (mission/culture/_____) and how our (product/service/_____) complements this?

3. Can you share an example of a time when a product or service made a significant (emotional/transformative/_____) impact on your organization?

4. How do you envision our (product/service/_____) playing a role in a story that not only solves problems but also evokes a strong (emotional response/connection/_____)?

5. What (emotional triggers/values/_____) should our narrative highlight to align with your organization's (goals/ethos/_____)?

6. In what ways can we showcase our solution as not just a tool but as a partner in achieving (emotional milestones/significant transformations/_____)?

7. How important is it for our narrative to include elements of (hope/empowerment/_____) that mirror your organization's journey?

8. What type of (success stories/testimonials/_____) would most effectively convey the emotional benefits of our (product/service/_____) to your team?

9. How can our narrative address and alleviate any (fears/concerns/_____) your team might have about adopting a new (solution/technology/_____)?

10. Can you identify any (emotional pain points/areas of resistance/_____) within your team that our narrative should aim to (address/overcome/_____)?

(2) Client to Salesperson:

1. How does your narrative ensure an emotional connection, not just a transactional relationship, with your (clients/customers/_____)?

2. Can you provide examples of how your (product/service/_____) has emotionally impacted other organizations in a positive way?

3. How do you customize your sales narrative to resonate with the unique (values/culture/_____) of each client?

4. In what ways do you gather (feedback/insights/_____) to continually adapt your narrative to maintain emotional engagement?

5. How do you balance factual information with emotional storytelling in your (sales approach/business/_____)?

6. How do you measure the effectiveness of emotional engagement in your narratives, and how does this influence client (decisions/loyalty/_____)?

7. What methods do you use to ensure your story resonates emotionally across different (audiences/cultures/_____)?

8. Can you share how you adapt your narrative when the initial emotional approach does not connect as expected with a (client/audience/_____)?

9. How do you incorporate (customer feedback/emotional insights/_____) into developing your sales narrative for greater impact?

10. In your experience, what emotional elements of a narrative have the most significant impact on (building trust/encouraging action/_____) from clients?

(3) Salesperson to Self:

1. Am I effectively incorporating (emotional engagement/storytelling/_____) into my sales narratives to create memorable experiences for my clients?

2. How can I better understand and tap into the (emotional drivers/values/_____) of my clients to make my narratives more compelling?

3. What (stories/testimonials/_____) can I collect that show the emotional impact of our (product/service/_____)?

4. In what areas do I need to improve to more effectively connect with clients on an (emotional/relational/_____) level?

5. How can I use client (feedback/success stories/_____) to refine and personalize the emotional appeal of our narratives?

(4) Salesperson to Colleagues/Internal Team:

1. How can we collaborate to enhance the emotional engagement of our narratives by sharing (client stories/successes/_____)?

2. What training can we undertake to better craft stories that connect with our clients' (hearts/minds/_____)?

3. How can we leverage (marketing materials/testimonials/_____) to support our narrative's emotional appeal?

4. In what ways can we ensure our narratives consistently reflect the (values/emotions/_____) that resonate with our target audience?

5. What mechanisms can we put in place to capture and use (client feedback/emotional responses/_____) to improve our narratives?

(5) Salesperson to External Stakeholders or Partners:

1. How can our partnership help to amplify the emotional resonance of our narratives with shared (values/missions/_____)?

2. Can you provide (insights/tools/_____) that can help us better connect with our clients on an (emotional/psychological/_____) level?

3. In what ways can you support us in gathering (stories/testimonials/_____) that highlight the emotional impact of our solutions?

4. How do your (products/services/_____) complement our narrative in creating a stronger emotional connection with our clients?

5. What strategies have you found effective in creating narratives that not only inform but also emotionally engage (clients/customers/_____)?

6. POSITIONING FOR DIFFERENTIATION

A.   MARKET POSITIONING ANALYSIS:

These questions aim to sharpen your service or product's market positioning. They prompt a deep dive into distinguishing your offering, aligning it with client expectations, and leveraging competitive advantages. By focusing on unique selling points, client-centric differentiation, and the dynamic market landscape, you'll better communicate value and adjust strategies based on feedback. This method is crafted to elevate your product's standing and appeal in the competitive market efficiently.

(1) Salesperson to Client:

1. How can we better communicate our product's (unique selling propositions/competitive advantages/_____) to align with your (needs/goals/_____)?

2. What aspects of our (product/service/_____) differentiation matter most to you in your decision-making process?

3. Can you share insights on how our (unique selling propositions/features/_____) could address your current (challenges/requirements/_____) more effectively?

4. How do you perceive our (products/services/_____) compared to (competitors/alternative solutions/_____) in terms of (value/innovation/_____)?

5. What (feedback/suggestions/_____) do you have for us to enhance our market positioning to better serve your (needs/preferences/_____)?

6. In what ways can we illustrate our product's unique position in the market to more clearly show its (benefits/impact/_____) on your operations?

7. How important is it for our (marketing/sales/_____) messages to highlight specific (value/benefits/_____) that differentiate us from our competitors?

8. What (information/resources/_____) can we provide to help you better understand our market positioning and (value proposition/contribution/_____)?

9. Can you identify any (gaps/missed opportunities/_____) in our current market positioning that we could improve to meet your (specific needs/challenges/_____)?

10. How do you suggest we tailor our communication to better highlight our (product/service's/_____) unique (features/advantages/_____) in a way that resonates with your organization?

(2) Client to Salesperson:

1. How do you define your product's unique selling propositions in the context of my industry's specific (challenges/needs/_____)?

2. What evidence or (case studies/data/_____) can you provide to support your claims of differentiation in the market?

3. How does your product's positioning reflect an understanding of (our company's unique needs/the competitive landscape/_____)?

4. In what ways have you adapted your (product/service/_____) to remain (competitive/relevant/_____) in response to market changes?

5. Can you explain how your product's (features/benefits/_____) directly address my most critical business (challenges/objectives/_____)?

6. How frequently do you (review/update/_____) your product's positioning to ensure it remains (relevant/competitive/_____) in the growing market?

7. What role does (customer feedback/market research/_____) play in shaping the positioning of your (product/service/_____)?

8. Can you detail how your service's (features/benefits/_____) directly contribute to solving industry-specific (problems/challenges/_____)?

9. How do you communicate your product's unique position to (new prospects/existing customers/_____) in a way that is both (informative/engaging/_____)?

10. What measures are in place to (educate/train/_____) your sales team about the nuances of your product's market positioning and its (advantages/benefits/_____) over competitors?

(3) Salesperson to Self:

1. Am I effectively leveraging our product's (unique selling propositions/competitive advantages/_____) in my sales narrative to differentiate from competitors?

2. How well do I understand and articulate the (value/impact/_____) our product brings to clients compared to the market alternatives?

3. What steps can I take to deepen my knowledge of our competitive landscape and our product's unique (position/value/_____) within it?

4. How can I better tailor my sales approach to highlight our product's (unique benefits/specific advantages/_____) that resonate with my target audience?

5. In what areas do I need improvement to communicate our market positioning more convincingly and (benefits/differentiators/_____) to potential clients?

(4) Salesperson to Colleagues/Internal Team:

1. How can we collaborate to strengthen our understanding and communication of our product's (market positioning/value/_____)?

2. What (strategies/action plans/_____) can we develop to more effectively differentiate our (product/service/_____) in our sales and marketing materials?

3. How can we better use (customer feedback/market analysis/_____) to refine our positioning strategy and highlight our competitive advantages?

4. In what ways can we support each other in staying informed about (competitive movements/market trends/_____) that affect our product's positioning?

5. What (training/resources/_____) do we need to better articulate our product's unique selling propositions and competitive differentiation to clients?

(5) Salesperson to External Stakeholders or Partners:

1. How can our partnership enhance our product's (market positioning/competitive edge/_____) through shared (expertise/resources/_____)?

2. In what ways can you provide insights or data that help us refine our (understanding/marketing efforts/_____) of our competitive advantage in the market?

3. Can you share how your organization successfully navigated market positioning challenges and what we can learn from it?

4. How do you suggest we leverage external (partnerships/collaborations/_____) to strengthen our product's differentiation in the market?

5. What (tools/strategies/_____) have you found effective in analyzing and enhancing product positioning that we could adopt or adapt?

B.   TAILORING THE STORY TO SEGMENTS:

These questions are crafted to enhance sales narratives, ensuring they resonate deeply with different market segments' unique needs and challenges. Tailoring stories to specific industry goals and preferences boosts the effectiveness of sales strategies. These queries facilitate creating personalized narratives that spotlight the most relevant value and benefits for each target group, thereby improving engagement and influencing decision-making processes.

(1) Salesperson to Client:

1. How can we adjust our (narrative/strategy/_____) to better align with the specific (challenges/goals/_____) of your industry segment?

2. What aspects of our (product/service/_____) are most relevant to your segment's unique (needs/preferences/_____)?

3. Can you provide insights into how we can make our sales story more compelling for your particular (market segment/business type/_____)?

4. How do differences in (industry contexts/customer behaviors/_____) within your segment influence your decision-making process?

5. In what ways can we highlight our product's (value/benefits/_____) to address the specific challenges faced by your (industry/sector/_____)?

6. What (information/examples/_____) would you find most useful in a customized sales narrative for your (segment/niche/_____)?

7. How do you suggest we tailor our message to resonate more deeply with the unique (values/culture/_____) of your market segment?

8. What (feedback/suggestions/_____) do you have for our approach to differentiating our (product/service/_____) in your market?

9. Can you share a story where a tailored sales approach significantly impacted your (perspective/decision/_____) positively?

10. How important is segment-specific customization in our sales narrative to your (evaluation process/purchasing decision/_____)?

(2) Client to Salesperson:

1. How does your company customize its sales narratives for different (customer segments/industries/_____)?

2. Can you show me examples of how your (product/service/_____) has been positioned differently for various market segments?

3. What methods do you use to ensure your sales narrative remains relevant across diverse (industries/customers/_____)?

4. How frequently do you (update/review/_____) your sales approach to adapt to changes (within my industry segment/in the macro-economic environment/_____)?

5. What success stories can you share about clients in my segment who have benefited from your tailored sales narrative?

6. How do you gather and use (customer feedback/industry insights/_____) to continuously refine your sales narrative for my segment?

7. What challenges have you encountered when customizing your narrative for diverse segments, and how have you overcome them?

8. Can you detail how your sales narrative adapts to the specific (pain points/goals/_____) of new market segments you enter?

9. How do you ensure that your narrative for my segment stays (current/relevant/_____) amidst rapidly changing industry trends?

10. What role does (technological innovation/market research/_____) play in keeping your segment-specific narratives (effective/engaging/_____)?

(3) Salesperson to Self:

1. Am I effectively identifying and leveraging the unique (needs/challenges/_____) of each customer segment in my sales narratives?

2. How can I improve my understanding of different market segments to better tailor our (product's/service's/_____) story?

3. What resources can I utilize to stay updated on the evolving (preferences/trends/_____) of each segment I target?

4. In what areas do I need further development to customize our narrative more skillfully for diverse (audiences/segments/_____)?

5. How can I measure the impact of our tailored sales narratives on (customer engagement/sales success/_____) in various segments?

(4) Salesperson to Colleagues/Internal Team:

1. How can we work together to gather (insights/data/_____) that will inform our tailored narratives for different customer segments?

2. What best practices can we establish for creating segment-specific sales narratives that resonate with each group's (needs/preferences/_____)?

3. How can we ensure consistency in our differentiation strategy while tailoring our narrative to various (segments/industries/_____)?

4. What feedback mechanisms can we put in place to evaluate the effectiveness of our tailored narratives across different (segments/markets/_____)?

5. Can we collaborate on developing a repository of (case studies/success stories/_____) that showcases our narrative's impact on different segments?

(5) Salesperson to External Stakeholders or Partners:

1. How can our partnerships enhance our ability to tailor sales narratives for specific (segments/industries/_____) effectively?

2. In what ways can you provide (support/resources/_____) to help us better understand and penetrate specific market segments?

3. Can you share (insights/trends/_____) from your experience that could help us refine our approach to different customer segments?

4. How do your (products/services/_____) complement our tailored narratives for various (customer segments/industries/_____)?

5. What collaborative opportunities exist for us to address jointly the unique challenges and opportunities within specific (segments/markets/_____)?

7. LEVERAGING STORYTELLING IN SALES CONVERTSAIONS

A.   INTEGRATING STORIES INTO SALES CONVERSATIONS:

These questions aim to weave storytelling into sales discussions, enriching the connection with clients' unique challenges and goals. Effective storytelling can transform sales interactions by aligning product impacts with client aspirations, integrating authentic success stories tailored to industry-specific needs. This approach seeks to ensure narratives resonate with clients' values, address concerns, and show the solution's potential, facilitating more engaging and meaningful sales conversations.

(1) Salesperson to Client:

1. How can we incorporate stories that (highlight/resonate with/_____) your specific (challenges/ambitions/_____) through our sales conversations?

2. What kind of (success stories/case studies/_____) would you find most relevant to your (industry/needs/_____)?

3. Can you share any (expectations/preferences/_____) for how storytelling should be integrated into our presentations to better engage your team?

4. In what ways can stories of our product's (impact/success/_____) in similar contexts help in addressing your (hesitations/questions/_____)?

5. How important is it for you that the stories we share align with your (values/corporate culture/_____)?

6. How can a story about our (product's/service's/_____) impact in a similar industry context help you envision its potential for your (organization/goals/_____)?

7. What type of narrative would make our solution more (appealing/memorable/_____) to your decision-making process?

8. Can you describe a past experience where a vendor's story significantly influenced your (purchase decision/strategy/_____)?

9. How do you prefer to see (customer testimonials/real-world examples/_____) integrated into sales discussions to better assess potential outcomes?

10. What (challenges/successes/_____) in your industry would you like to see reflected in the stories we share about our (products/services/_____)?

(2) Client to Salesperson:

1. Can you share a story where your product/service made a significant (difference/impact/_____) for a client with similar (needs/challenges/_____) as ours?

2. How do you tailor your storytelling to different (audiences/segments/_____), ensuring relevance and engagement?

3. What feedback have you received from other clients about the effectiveness of storytelling in (your sales process, their businesses/_____)?

4. How do you ensure the stories you tell are (authentic/credible/_____) and reflect real-world outcomes?

5. Can you demonstrate how your solution has evolved based on (customer stories/feedback/_____)?

6. How have other clients in my (industry/segment/_____) utilized your (product/service/_____) to overcome specific (challenges/growth barriers/_____)?

7. Can you provide an example of how your storytelling approach has adapted over time in response to (market changes/client feedback/_____)?

8. What is the most memorable (feedback/story/_____) you've received from a client about the impact of your (product/service/_____)?

9. How do you ensure that the stories you tell about your (products/services/_____) stay relevant and engaging for a diverse client base?

10. In your experience, what elements of a (sales story/business proposal/_____) are most effective in capturing the attention and interest of (prospective clients/your audience/_____)?

(3) Salesperson to Self:

1. Am I effectively using storytelling to make our (product/service/_____) more relatable and compelling to each client's (situation/needs/_____)?

2. How can I improve my storytelling skills to better engage clients and convey the (value/impact/_____) of our offerings?

3. What stories have resonated most with my clients, and how can I leverage similar narratives in future (conversations/negotiations/_____)?

4. How well do I integrate client (feedback/testimonials/_____) into my sales conversations as success stories?

5. In what areas could I use more (training/resources/_____) to enhance my ability to tell compelling stories that drive sales?

(4) Salesperson to Colleagues/Internal Team:

1. How can we collaborate to develop a library of (success stories/case studies/_____) that we can easily integrate into sales conversations?

2. What approaches can we share with our team for effectively incorporating storytelling into our sales approach?

3. How can we use storytelling to better highlight our product's (value/competitive advantages/_____)?

4. In what ways can we gather and use (client feedback/stories/_____) to continually enrich our sales narratives?

5. What (training/resources/_____) do we need to better equip our team for storytelling in sales?

(5) Salesperson to External Stakeholders or Partners:

1. How can our partnership provide unique (stories/content/_____) that enhance our sales narratives and distinguishes our (offerings/partnership/_____)?

2. Can you share (insights/data/_____) that we can use to create compelling stories for our sales conversations?

3. In what ways have your (products/services/_____) contributed to success stories that we can integrate into our narrative?

4. How do you suggest we adapt our storytelling approach when introducing your (products/services/_____) into our (solutions/business proposal/_____)?

5. What collaborative opportunities can we explore to create new success stories that resonate with our (target audiences/sales team/_____)?

B.   STORYTELLING TRAINING FOR SALES TEAMS:

These questions guide the enhancement of storytelling in sales, focusing on stories that resonate with clients' needs and aspirations. They explore training you to craft compelling narratives that highlight product benefits and align with clients' values. By incorporating client feedback and experiences, you become more engaging and persuasive. This approach highlights the significance of being real, pertinent, and customized in storytelling, aiming to strengthen client relationships and clearly communicate the value of what is being offered.

(1) Salesperson to Client:

1. How can stories of (transformation/success/_____) from similar clients enhance our presentation to meet your (expectations/needs/_____)?

2. What type of storytelling do you find most (engaging/credible/_____) when discussing potential solutions for your (challenges/goals/_____)?

3. Can you provide examples of (problems/challenges/_____) that you'd like to see solved through our storytelling in sales conversations?

4. How important is it for you to hear stories that show our (flexibility/innovation/_____) in adapting solutions to fit customer needs?

5. What storytelling format do you prefer during sales presentations: (narratives/case studies/_____)?

6. How can we better incorporate your (feedback/visions/_____) into our stories to ensure they resonate with your (values/goals/_____)?

7. What specific aspects of our (products/services/_____) would you like to see highlighted through storytelling in our future conversations?

8. Can you identify a type of story (success story/challenge overcome/_____) that would significantly influence your (purchasing decisions/decision-making process/_____)?

9. How do you feel about incorporating interactive elements into our stories, such as (customer testimonials/interactive demos/_____)?

10. What storytelling approach do you believe would be most effective in conveying the (long-term benefits/ROI/_____) of our solution to your stakeholders?

(2) Client to Salesperson:

1. Can you share how your sales team's storytelling training has improved their ability to communicate the value of your (products/services/_____)?

2. What techniques do your salespeople use to weave in stories that resonate with a diverse range of clients like (ours/technology firms/_____)?

3. How do you ensure the stories told by your sales team are both (relevant/authentic/_____) to our specific (industry/challenges/_____)?

4. Can you give an example of a story that dramatically changed a client's (perception/decision-making process/_____)?

5. How do you tailor stories for different segments within the same industry to address their unique (needs/challenges/_____)?

6. How do you personalize your stories to connect with clients who have unique or niche (requirements/preferences/_____)?

7. What's the most memorable feedback you've received from a client about the impact of a story shared during the sales process?

8. How does your team stay updated with relevant stories that reflect the latest (industry trends/product updates/_____)?

9. Can you describe a situation where storytelling directly contributed to overcoming (objections/skepticism/_____) from a client?

10. How do you ensure that the stories your sales team shares are consistently (aligned with/reflective of/_____) your brand's message and values?

(3) Salesperson to Self:

1. Am I effectively using storytelling techniques learned in training to connect with my clients on a (personal/emotional/_____) level?

2. How can I improve my storytelling to make our (product's/service's/_____) benefits more tangible for clients?

3. What feedback have I received on my storytelling, and how can I use it to refine my approach for different (audiences/scenarios/_____)?

4. Do I clearly understand the (structure/themes/_____) of effective sales stories that resonate with my target audience?

5. How can I better integrate storytelling into my sales conversations to highlight our (value/competitive advantages/_____)?

(4) Salesperson to Colleagues/Internal Team:

1. How can we collectively develop a bank of compelling stories that highlight our (unique value/impact/_____) across different industries?

2. In what ways can we share and learn from each other's experiences to enhance our storytelling skills in sales conversations?

3. What storytelling techniques have you found (most/least/_____) effective in engaging clients and how can we incorporate them into our team's training?

4. How can we better support each other in tailoring stories to resonate with specific client segments or industries?

5. What (tools/resources/_____) have been most helpful in improving your ability to integrate storytelling into sales (presentations/materials/_____)?

(5) Salesperson to External Stakeholders or Partners:

1. How can our partnership enrich the storytelling we use in sales conversations with real-world examples of (collaboration/success/_____)?

2. Can you provide insights or data that can help us craft more intriguing stories for our target (markets/audiences/_____)?

3. What stories from our partnership have had a significant impact on clients, and how can we leverage these in future sales narratives?

4. How do you suggest we adapt our storytelling training to incorporate the benefits of our partnership into our sales team's narratives?

5. What feedback have you received from (former clients/the market/_____) that could help us refine our storytelling approach to better meet client expectations?

8. ADDRESSING OBJECTIONS AND CONCERNS

A.   PREPARATION FOR OBJECTIONS:

Preparing for objections is crucial in sales, focusing on preemptively addressing client concerns about pricing, quality, and implementation. These questions help you articulate the value proposition and unique advantages of your offerings, comparing them favorably against competitors. Effective handling of these concerns strengthens client trust and supports their decision-making, highlighting the importance of understanding client hesitations and collaboratively working towards overcoming budgetary and technological constraints.

(1) Salesperson to Client:

1. How can we address your concerns regarding the (price/value/_____) of our solution effectively?

2. What information can I provide to reassure you about t(he (quality/durability/_____) of our product?

3. How do you see our (product/service/_____) solving your (specific problem/need/_____)?

4. In what ways can we show the (long-term value/ROI/_____) of our solution to your satisfaction?

5. Can you share any hesitations you have about the (implementation process/technology integration/_____)?

6. What comparisons have you made with other solutions, and how do we stand regarding (features/support/_____)?

7. How important is (scalability/flexibility/_____) in your (decision-making process, discussion with your senior management/_____) for choosing a solution?

8. What additional (information/support/_____) can I provide to help you understand the (benefits/unique advantages/_____) of our product better?

9. In discussing our solution, what aspects do you find (most/least/_____) compelling, and where do you see (concerns/gaps/_____)?

10. How can we work together to overcome any (budgetary/timeframe/_____) constraints (you/your colleagues/_____) are facing?

(2) Client to Salesperson:

1. How does your (product/service/_____) compare to (competitors/alternative solutions/_____) in terms of (price/quality/_____)?

2. Can you explain how your solution addresses our specific (needs/challenges/_____) more effectively than others?

3. What (guarantees/assurances/_____) do you offer regarding (product reliability/service support/_____)?

4. How flexible is your (pricing model/proposal/_____) to accommodate our (budget/financial constraints/_____)?

5. What is your (implementation/support/_____) plan to ensure a smooth transition to your product?

6. Can you provide examples of how your solution has helped others with similar (problems/requirements/_____)?

7. What are the most common (objections/problems/_____) you hear about your product, and how do you (address/overcome/_____) them?

8. How does (your company/you/_____) stay ahead in terms of (innovation/technology updates/_____)?

9. What (training/resources/_____) do you provide to ensure we maximize the use of your (product/support team/_____)?

10. How do you (measure/ensure/_____) customer (satisfaction/success/_____) with your solution?

(3) Salesperson to Self:

1. Have I thoroughly prepared for potential objections to our (pricing/technology/_____)?

2. How confident am I in my ability to articulate the (value proposition/ROI/_____) of our solution?

3. What strategies can I employ to better (understand/address/_____) client concerns about (compatibility/integration/_____)?

4. In what areas do I need more (knowledge/resources/_____) to effectively counter objections related to (product limitations/service offerings/_____)?

5. How can I improve my (listening/negotiation/_____) skills to better address and overcome objections?

(4) Salesperson to Colleagues/Internal Team:

1. How have we successfully addressed customer concerns about (cost-effectiveness/product features/_____) in the past?

2. What insights can you share about overcoming objections related to (market competition/technology advancements/_____)?

3. Can you provide examples of how our solution has met the (specific needs/expectations/_____) of similar clients?

4. What additional (training/materials/_____) can help me prepare for objections about (usability/integration/_____)?

5. How can we ensure that we communicate our (pricing strategy/value proposition/_____) effectively to address common objections?

(5) Salesperson to External Stakeholders or Partners:

1. How can our partnership enhance the (value proposition/competitive edge/_____) of our offering in the face of objections?

2. What support can you offer in terms of (training/resources/_____) to help address potential client concerns?

3. How do you suggest we handle objections about (industry standards/technological compatibility/_____)?

4. Can you provide examples of (success stories/case studies/_____) where your company transformed objections into (strengths/opportunities/_____)?

5. In what ways can we leverage our partnership to reinforce confidence in the (reliability/efficiency/_____) of our solution?

B.   OBJECTION HANDLING TECHNIQUES:

Effective objection handling is pivotal in sales, aiming to reassure clients about the value, integration, and effectiveness of offerings. This set of questions is designed to guide you in confidently addressing client concerns, emphasizing the importance of understanding hesitations, demonstrating tailored benefits, and showcasing long-term value. By employing strategies like showcasing successful case studies and offering detailed support, you can build stronger client relationships and affirm the worth of your solutions.

(1) Salesperson to Client:

1. How can I help you feel more comfortable about the (cost/benefit/_____) of our solution?

2. What concerns do you have about (integrating/using/_____) our product in your (daily operations/business/_____)?

3. Can you share what aspects of our (service/product/_____) you're feeling uncertain about?

4. How have you addressed similar challenges in the past with other (vendors/products/_____)?

5. What information can I provide that would ease your concerns regarding (implementation/support/_____)?

6. In what ways can I show the (effectiveness/value/_____) of our solution to your (specific needs/clients/_____)?

7. What specific (features/offerings/_____) are you comparing when looking at our solution and others?

8. Can we explore a (case study/testimonial/_____) where a similar objection was successfully overcome?

9. How important is (scalability/customization/_____) for you in selecting a solution, and how can we address that?

10. What would make you feel more confident about the (ROI/long-term benefits/_____) of our product?

(2) Client to Salesperson:

1. How does your solution offer better (value/ROI/_____) compared to other options we're considering?

2. Can you clarify how your (support services/implementation process/_____) works in detail?

3. What evidence can you provide to show your product will meet our (specific need/requirement/_____)?

4. How flexible are you on (pricing/terms/_____) to fit our budget constraints?

5. What are the long-term benefits of partnering with your company beyond (the immediate solution/available resources)?

6. Can you address our concerns about (data security/product compatibility/_____) with your solution?

7. How does your company stay ahead with (updates/innovations/_____) in your product offerings?

8. What kind of (training/support/_____) do you offer to ensure we maximize the use of your (product/service/_____)?

9. Can you explain how your product has developed in response to (customer feedback/industry trends/_____)?

10. How do you ensure (customer satisfaction/ongoing support/_____) post-purchase?

(3) Salesperson to Self:

1. How well do I understand the (objections/concerns/_____) from clients, and how can I prepare better?

2. What can I learn from previous (successes/failures/_____) to handle similar objections?

3. How can I improve my (listening/empathy/_____) skills to better connect with and reassure clients?

4. What additional (knowledge/resources/_____) do I need to address client objections more effectively?

5. How can I better use the "feel, felt, found" technique in my future (conversations/presentations/_____)?

(4) Salesperson to Colleagues/Internal Team:

1. Can you share (insights/tactics/_____) that have worked for you in overcoming (price objections/product fit concerns/_____)?

2. How can we collaborate to enhance our (objection handling strategies/knowledge base/_____)?

3. What resources or (training materials/success stories/_____) can help me better address client objections?

4. How can we stay updated on (product improvements/competitive intelligence/_____) to preemptively address objections?

5. What role can each department play in creating a more compelling (value proposition/objection handling framework/_____)?

(5) Salesperson to External Stakeholders or Partners:

1. How can we leverage our partnership to address common objections regarding (product compatibility/overall value/_____)?

2. What success stories from our partnership can I share to overcome objections related to (experience/track record/_____)?

3. How do you suggest we handle objections that concern your part of the (solution/service/_____)?

4. What (tools/resources/_____) do you offer that could help us better prepare for and address objections?

5. Can you provide insights into (industry trends/common business challenges/_____) that help address objections related to (innovation/technology advancement/_____)?

C.   ADDITIONAL CONSIDERATIONS:

Addressing client objections is key to sales success. These questions help you understand and mitigate concerns about cost, integration, and overall value. By offering demos, sharing success stories, and aligning solutions with client goals, you can clearly articulate your product's benefits. This strategy not only addresses concerns but also showcases long-term advantages, encouraging clients to consider implementation. It's about turning challenges into opportunities for demonstrating the unique value of the solution.

(1) Salesperson to Client:

1. How can our solution improve your (workflow/productivity/_____) by addressing the current challenges you're facing?

2. Can you see the (benefits/value/_____) our solution offers in overcoming the concerns you mentioned?

3. What if we could show you how others in your situation have (benefited/transformed/_____) their (process/results/_____) by choosing our solution?

4. Would a (demo/free trial/_____) help illustrate how our solution can meet your needs effectively?

5. How do you feel about moving forward if we can address your concerns regarding (cost/effectiveness/_____) satisfactorily?

6. Can we explore how our solution aligns with your (goals/objectives/_____) despite the initial objections?

7. Would testimonials from similar clients who had the same concerns help in reassessing our solution's (value/fit/_____)?

8. How does incorporating our solution with a (flexible payment plan/additional support/_____) sound to ease your budget concerns?

9. What features are most critical to you, and how can we ensure our solution provides the (value/utility/_____) you're looking for?

10. After addressing your major concerns, what are the next steps you see in possibly (implementing/adopting/_____) our solution?

(2) Client to Salesperson:

1. What assurances can you provide that your solution will address our (specific concern/requirement/_____)?

2. How have other companies in our industry benefited from your solution in terms of (ROI/efficiency/_____)?

3. Can you provide (evidence/case studies/_____) that show your solution's effectiveness in (resolving specific objections/addressing certain needs/_____)?

4. How does your company plan to support us in overcoming the (implementation/operation/_____) challenges?

5. What are the long-term (benefits/cost savings/_____) of your solution compared to the initial investment?

6. How do you differentiate your (customer service/support/_____) from competitors, especially when addressing client concerns?

7. Can you explain how your solution is (adaptable/future-proof/_____) to changing industry needs and challenges?

8. What flexibility do you offer in (pricing/terms/_____) to accommodate our budgetary constraints?

9. How quickly can we expect to see results after implementing your solution in terms of (productivity gains/cost reduction/_____)?

10. What is your process for (collecting/implementing/_____) customer feedback on your (product/service/_____)?

(3) Salesperson to Self:

1. How effectively am I using positive framing to highlight the (benefits/solutions/_____) of our product?

2. What additional (evidence/testimonials/_____) can I incorporate to strengthen my responses to objections?

3. How can I improve my skills in building a bridge from objections to solutions, particularly in areas of (technology/price/_____)?

4. Have I mastered the art of the trial close, and how can I better gauge a prospect's readiness to (proceed/make a decision/_____)?

5. What new (strategies/techniques/_____) can I adopt to turn objections into opportunities for (engagement/sales/_____)?

(4) Salesperson to Colleagues/Internal Team:

1. Can you share how you successfully transitioned a conversation from focusing on objections to discussing our solution's (benefits/features/_____)?

2. What (case studies/testimonials/_____) have you found most effective in addressing common objections about our (product/service/_____)?

3. How can we ensure that all team members are equipped with the latest (product updates/success stories/_____) in order to confidently handle objections?

4. What new evidence or (research/findings/_____) can we leverage to reinforce the value of our solution during objection handling?

5. How can we better collaborate to create a comprehensive knowledge base that includes (FAQs/objection handling scripts/_____) for sales conversations?

(5) Salesperson to External Stakeholders or Partners:

1. How can our partnership provide additional (value/support/_____) to clients who have specific objections about (cost/implementation/_____)?

2. What success stories from our partnership can we share to show how we've jointly addressed (industry-specific concerns/client objections/_____)?

3. How do you suggest we handle objections regarding the (integration/compatibility/_____) of our combined solutions?

4. Can you provide any (data/insights/_____) that we can use to back up our claims and strengthen our position against objections?

5. What (training/materials/_____) are available through our partnership that can help our sales team become more proficient in objection handling?

9. CLOSING TECHNIQUES

A.   TRIAL CLOSES:

Trial closes serve as a litmus test within sales conversations, enabling you to evaluate a prospect's interest and address any hesitations by asking targeted questions about the solution's fit, features, and value. This approach aids in uncovering and mitigating potential objections, ensuring the solution aligns with the client's goals. Effectively used, trial closes help smoothly transition discussions toward finalizing a decision, optimizing the path to a successful sale.

(1) Salesperson to Client:

1. How do you feel about the (features/benefits/_____) we've discussed today?

2. Do you see how our solution could (solve your problem/enhance your process/_____) based on what we've covered?

3. Are there any (features/benefits/_____) we discussed that you'd like more information on?

4. On a scale of 1-10, how would you rate your interest in (implementing/adopting/_____) our solution?

5. Can you see any potential challenges in integrating our solution with your current (systems/processes/_____)?

6. What are your thoughts on the (pricing/payment plans/_____) options we've outlined?

7. Is there anything preventing you from (moving forward/deciding/_____) today?

8. How does our solution align with your current (goals/strategic objectives/_____)?

9. What additional information can I provide to help you make a (decision/next step/_____)?

10. Are you ready to take the next step and (schedule a demo/sign up for a trial/_____)?

(2) Client to Salesperson:

1. Can you provide more details on how your solution addresses our specific concern about (cost-effectiveness/compatibility/_____)?

2. How does your (support/warranty/_____) policy work in practice?

3. What are the next steps if we decide to (move forward/proceed with a purchase/_____)?

4. How have other clients in our industry benefited from using your (product/service/_____)?

5. Can you explain the (implementation/training/_____) process in more detail?

6. What flexibility do you offer in terms of (customization/integration/_____) to fit our unique (needs/goals/_____)?

7. How quickly can we expect to see (results/benefits/_____) from implementing your solution?

8. What are the long-term (costs/savings/_____) associated with your solution?

9. How does your company handle (updates/upgrades/_____) for the solution?

10. Can you share a (case study/referral/_____) where your solution solved a problem like ours?

(3) Salesperson to Self:

1. Have I effectively communicated the (value/benefits/_____) of our solution throughout the presentation?

2. What cues (verbal/non-verbal/_____) did I notice that show the client's interest or readiness?

3. How can I improve my ability to gauge a prospect's (interest/readiness/_____) through trial closes?

4. Did I address all the client's questions and concerns to their satisfaction, leaving no (doubts/uncertainties/_____)?

5. What feedback did I receive today that can help me refine my (presentation/closing technique/_____) for future opportunities?

(4) Salesperson to Colleagues/Internal Team:

1. What strategies have you found effective for identifying a prospect's (readiness/interest/_____) during presentations?

2. Can you share examples of trial closes that have successfully moved prospects towards a decision?

3. How do you ensure that the client fully understands the (features/benefits/_____) of our solution?

4. What (training/coaching sessions/_____) are available to improve our skills in (closing/objection handling/_____)?

5. How can we better collaborate to prepare for and address potential (objections/questions/_____) during the closing phase?

(5) Salesperson to External Stakeholders or Partners:

1. How can we work together to enhance the closing process for clients, particularly to provide (evidence/testimonials/_____)?

2. What insights can you offer on the most effective trial closes you've seen in our (industry/country/_____)?

3. Can you provide (case studies/examples/_____) where our combined solutions have been a decisive factor in closing a deal?

4. How do your (products/operations/_____) complement ours in a way that strengthens the (value proposition/closing argument/_____)?

5. What (training/support/_____) can you offer to help our team become more effective in closing sales?

B. CLOSING STRATEGIES:

Closing strategies are crucial for finalizing sales, ensuring solutions align with clients' objectives. This set of questions helps confirm the solution's fit, tackle last-minute concerns, and encourage clients towards a positive decision. Tailored to gauge readiness and emphasize value, these strategies aim for a successful conclusion by highlighting mutual benefits. Through careful questioning, you can navigate towards agreement, reinforcing the solution's advantages and smoothing the path to a committed partnership.

(1) Salesperson to Client:

1. Based on our discussions, how well do you feel our solution aligns with your (objectives/needs/_____)?

2. Considering the (benefits/features/_____) we've covered, what stands out most to you as a reason to proceed?

3. Can we go over any remaining questions you have about how our solution addresses your (specific concern/requirement/_____)?

4. How do you see our (product/service/_____) improving your (workflow/efficiency/_____) compared to your current solution?

5. Would you agree that the value we offer justifies the investment, especially considering the (ROI/cost savings/_____)?

6. Are you ready to take the next step and enhance your (operations/strategy/_____) with our solution?

7. How does the idea of proceeding with a (pilot program/full implementation/_____) of our solution sound to you?

8. Can we summarize the key points that make our solution the right fit for your (business/challenges/_____)?

9. What are your thoughts on finalizing the decision today to start realizing the benefits of our (product/service/_____) sooner?

10. Do you feel confident moving forward, knowing our (support team/product roadmap/_____) is in place to ensure your success?

(2) Client to Salesperson:

1. Can you provide a final summary of how your solution outperforms others in terms of (features/benefits/_____)?

2. What guarantees can you offer that your (product/service/_____) will deliver the promised (results/outcomes/_____)?

3. How flexible are you on (pricing/terms/_____) to accommodate our budget and make this decision easier?

4. Can you explain once more how your (customer service/support/_____) works after the purchase?

5. What's the first step we need to take if we decide to proceed with your (solution/offer/_____) today?

6. How quickly can we expect to implement your solution and see tangible (results/improvements/_____)?

7. Can you detail the (training/onboarding/_____) process for our (team/senior management/_____) once we decide to move forward?

8. What have other clients said about their experience transitioning to your (product/service/_____)?

9. How does your solution provide (scalability/flexibility/_____) as our business grows and evolves?

10. Are there any (promotions/discounts/_____) available if we make a decision by (a certain date/_____)?

(3) Salesperson to Self:

1. Have I tailored my closing approach to match the prospect's (personality/needs/_____) effectively?

2. What signs of readiness did I observe, and how did I adapt my closing strategy to these indicators?

3. How can I improve my application of different closing techniques, such as (assumptive/urgency/_____), in future sales conversations?

4. Did I effectively summarize the key benefits and address all concerns before attempting to close?

5. How can I better prepare for future (sales meetings/team meetings/_____) to ensure a stronger, more confident close?

(4) Salesperson to Colleagues/Internal Team:

1. What successful closing strategies have you used in situations similar to (mine/this recent case/_____)?

2. Can we review my closing approach and identify areas for (improvement/optimization/_____)?

3. How do you handle objections that come up during the closing phase, especially regarding (pricing/value proposition/_____)?

4. What (resources/tools/_____) have you found most effective in supporting your (summary/balance sheet/_____) close?

5. Can we role-play different closing scenarios to enhance our skills in (direct closing/consultative closing/_____)?

(5) Salesperson to External Stakeholders or Partners:

1. How can we collaborate to strengthen our closing arguments, particularly using (testimonials/case studies/_____)?

2. What insights can you share on overcoming last-minute hesitations during the close, especially with (specific objections/competitive comparisons/_____)?

3. Can you provide examples of how your support has helped close deals, particularly in (challenging/niche/_____) markets?

4. How do your offerings complement ours in a way that we can leverage during the closing phase to highlight (combined value/additional benefits/_____)?

5. What (training/support/_____) do you offer that can help our team become more proficient in applying different closing strategies?

C.   NEGOTIATION:

Negotiating effectively is crucial for sealing deals that satisfy both parties. These questions are designed to guide negotiations by aligning our offerings with the client's financial plans and specific needs. They help explore adjustments, discuss terms, and highlight our solution's value, aiming for mutual benefits. This approach fosters open dialogue about concerns, preferences, and potential customizations, ensuring proposals are compelling and agreeable, and paving the way for successful partnerships.

(1) Salesperson to Client:

1. How do you see our (product/service/_____) fitting into your current (budget/plan/_____)?

2. Which of the presented options best aligns with your needs, considering (price/delivery terms/_____)?

3. In terms of customization, what specific aspects of our offer would you like to adjust to better meet your (objectives/requirements/_____)?

4. Can we explore a solution that addresses both our interests, particularly focusing on (pricing/terms/_____)?

5. How do you determine if our (product/service/_____) is worth the investment?

6. What are your primary concerns regarding our (pricing/delivery options/_____), and how can we address these?

7. Are there specific (payment terms/service levels/_____) that you're looking for that we can discuss further?

8. How important is (flexibility/scalability/_____) in our solution to (meet your needs/achieve your goals/_____)?

9. What would make our proposal more competitive to you, especially in terms of (cost savings/efficiency gains/_____)?

10. Could we agree on a (trial period/special discount/_____) that would allow you to assess our solution's impact without full commitment?

(2) Client to Salesperson:

1. What are your most flexible terms for (pricing/payment/_____) that you can offer?

2. How does your solution provide a better (ROI/value/_____) compared to your competitors?

3. Can you offer any additional (services/support/_____) at the current price point?

4. What assurances can you provide regarding (delivery times/product quality/_____)?

5. Are there options for scaling up the service as our needs grow, especially regarding (cost/terms/_____)?

6. How customizable is your solution to our specific (industry/operational/_____) challenges?

7. What is the process for negotiating terms on (volume discounts/long-term contracts/_____)?

8. Can you detail the (warranty/guarantee/_____) terms for your product/service?

9. What are the possibilities for (deferred payments/additional training/_____) included in the package?

10. How do you ensure a win-win outcome in negotiations, especially concerning (after-sales service/upgrade paths/_____)?

(3) Salesperson to Self:

1. Have I clearly identified and communicated the unique (value/advantages/_____) of our offer?

2. What are my non-negotiables in this deal, and how well have I communicated these boundaries?

3. How can I better prepare for negotiations to ensure flexibility without compromising (profitability/values/_____)?

4. What additional (options/alternatives/_____) can I propose to create more customized solutions for clients?

5. How effectively am I listening to client needs and responding with (win-win solutions/better proposals/_____), especially concerning (terms/conditions/_____)?

(4) Salesperson to Colleagues/Internal Team:

1. What has been your experience in negotiating (pricing/terms/_____) with similar clients, and what strategies worked best?

2. Can we review past negotiations that led to successful outcomes, particularly those involving (custom offers/flexible pricing/_____)?

3. How do we ensure that our negotiation practices align with our overall (brand values/strategic goals/_____)?

4. What (data/common connections/_____) can we leverage to improve our negotiation outcomes, especially for (complex deals/high-value contracts/_____)?

5. How can we better support each other in negotiations to ensure we're offering the most (competitive/flexible/_____) solutions?

(5) Salesperson to External Stakeholders or Partners:

1. How can our partnership enhance our negotiation capabilities, particularly with (joint offers/special discounts/_____)?

2. What (strategies/counter arguments/_____) have you found effective in negotiations that we could apply, especially in terms of (pricing flexibility/service customization/_____)?

3. Can you share (insights/trends/_____) that might affect our negotiation strategies, especially related to (market demands/client expectations/_____)?

4. How do we leverage our combined strengths in negotiations to present a unified and compelling (value proposition/offer/_____)?

5. What (training/support/_____) do you offer that could help us (negotiate better deals/build long-term client relationships/_____)?

D.   ADDITIONAL CONSIDERATIONS:

Closing techniques extend beyond the sale, focusing on nurturing ongoing client relationships and engagement. These questions aim to keep clients updated, gather feedback for improvement, and ensure consistent follow-up, fostering long-term connections. They highlight the value of staying attuned to client needs, offering relevant updates, and soliciting referrals, all while maintaining continuous engagement. This strategy promotes sustained client satisfaction and opens avenues for future opportunities through regular communication and added value.

(1) Salesperson to Client:

1. How can we stay in touch to ensure you're informed about (future improvements/new offerings/_____) that might better meet your needs?

2. What's the best way for us to follow up with you, ensuring we can address any (new challenges/requirements/_____) that arise?

3. How do you prefer to receive updates about our (products/services/_____), so you remain aware of how we can support your (goals/pain-points/_____)?

4. Can we schedule a (follow-up call/review meeting/_____) to discuss how your needs might have changed and how we can assist?

5. Would you be open to receiving (industry insights/case studies/_____) that demonstrate the ongoing value we provide to clients like yourself?

6. After reflecting on our discussion, what additional information can I provide to help you see the (benefits/value/_____) of our solution?

7. How can we improve our offer to make it more aligned with your (budget/strategic goals/_____) in the (present/future/_____)?

8. Is there a (colleague/another department/_____) within your organization who might benefit from learning about our (solutions/services/_____)?

9. What feedback can you share about our negotiation and proposal process to help us serve you better in the future?

10. Would you find value in a (newsletter/webinar series/_____) that covers (trends/best practices/_____) related to (your industry/our solutions/_____)?

(2) Client to Salesperson:

1. What options do we have if we decide to proceed with your solution later?

2. Can you provide (examples/case scenarios/_____) of how your solution has developed to meet client needs over time?

3. How do you typically work with clients post-sale to (ensure satisfaction/address any concerns/_____)?

4. What is your process for (collecting/implementing/_____) client's feedback on your (product/service/_____)?

5. Are there any upcoming (product updates/special offers/_____) that we should know if we decide to wait?

(3) Salesperson to Self:

1. How effectively am I (developing/executing/_____) follow-up plans for prospects who initially decide against a sale?

2. What (strategies/operation procedure/_____) can I implement to better reassure customers post-close, minimizing buyer's remorse?

3. How can I more effectively solicit referrals from satisfied clients, expanding my (network/potential client base/_____)?

4. What lessons have I learned from (negotiations/meetings/_____) that didn't result in an immediate sale, and how can I apply them in the future?

5. How can I improve my approach to (setting/communicating/_____) boundaries during negotiations to ensure profitable and satisfactory outcomes?

(4) Salesperson to Colleagues/Internal Team:

1. What has been your most effective (strategy/elevator speech/_____) for maintaining engagement with prospects who didn't close on the first attempt?

2. Can we share (best practices/strategies/_____) for post-close engagement that (reassures clients/fosters long-term relationships/_____)?

3. How can we better leverage client feedback from (closed deals/non-closed deals/_____) to refine our (sales tactics/negotiation tactics/_____)?

4. What (insights/tools/_____) have you found most useful in generating referrals from our existing customer base?

5. How do we ensure our follow-up with non-closed prospects (is consistent/adds value/_____), keeping the door open for future opportunities?

(5) Salesperson to External Stakeholders or Partners:

1. How can we collaborate to provide ongoing value to our (current clients/prospects/_____)who haven't yet decided to purchase?

2. What insights can you share on best practices for follow-up that nurtures prospects towards a future sale?

3. Can you provide case (studies/data/_____) that support the long-term benefits of our solution, which I can share with undecided prospects?

4. What joint efforts can we undertake to reassure new customers of their decision, enhancing post-close satisfaction?

5. How can our partnership facilitate a more robust referral generation process, benefiting both our organizations?

10. POST-SALE ENGAGEMENT

A.   FOLLOW-UP:

These questions facilitate effective post-sale follow-up by assessing customer satisfaction, addressing concerns, and identifying opportunities for additional support or upgrades. The goal is to solidify customer relationships, enhance their experience with the product or service, and encourage loyalty and recommendations. This structured approach emphasizes the value of ongoing engagement, leveraging feedback for continuous improvement, and ensuring customers fully benefit from their purchase, ultimately contributing to sustained business success and growth.

(1) Salesperson to Client:

1. How has your experience been with our (product/service/_____) since your (purchase/last order/_____)?

2. What can we do to support you further in getting the most value out of your (investment/purchase/_____)?

3. Are there any (questions/concerns/_____) you have about the (features/implementation/_____) that we can address?

4. How would you rate your satisfaction with our (onboarding process/customer service/_____), and what improvements would you suggest?

5. Can we schedule a follow-up call to discuss any additional (needs/feedback/_____) you have regarding our (product/service/_____)?

6. Is there anything specific you'd like to learn more about to maximize your use of our (solution/technology/_____)?

7. Have you encountered any (challenges/issues/_____) with our (product/service/_____) that we can help resolve?

8. Would you be interested in receiving information about (new features/upgrades/_____) related to your purchase?

9. How likely are you to recommend our (product/service/_____) to others, and why?

10. What additional (resources/training/_____) can we provide to enhance your experience with our solution?

(2) Client to Salesperson:

1. Can you provide more detailed guidance on how to use (specific feature/aspect/_____) of your product?

2. What are the next steps if I need (additional support/more information/_____) on the service I purchased?

3. How do I provide feedback on my buying experience and the (product/service/_____) satisfaction?

4. Are there any upcoming (updates/extensions/_____) to the product I should know?

5. How can I get in touch with customer service quickly for (urgent issues/questions/_____)?

6. Can you outline the steps for (optimizing/maximizing/) the use of your solution based on our current (strategy/operations/)?

7. Can you detail the process for addressing (technical issues/unexpected challenges/) that may arise with your (software/hardware/)?

8. In terms of (product updates/new features/), what can we expect in the upcoming (months/quarters/_____), and how will they enhance our (efficiency/productivity/_____)?

9. How does your (customer service/support team/_____) handle (urgent inquiries/critical issues/_____), and what are the typical response times?

10. Can you provide case studies or examples of how similar clients have successfully (expanded/optimized/_____) their use of your (product/service/_____) over time?

(3) Salesperson to Self:

1. Have I effectively established a routine for follow-up that ensures (customer satisfaction/loyalty/_____)?

2. What have I learned from customer feedback that can improve my (sales approach/service delivery/_____)?

3. How can I better personalize my (follow-up messages/call script/_____) to enhance the customer's post-purchase experience?

4. What additional (training/resources/_____) do I need to address common post-sale (questions/concerns/_____) more effectively?

5. How can I more effectively use customer feedback to advocate for (product improvements/customer experience enhancements/_____) internally?

(4) Salesperson to Colleagues/Internal Team:

1. What best practices can we share about post-sale follow-up that have led to increased (customer satisfaction/expanded sales/_____)?

2. How can we streamline our onboarding process to make it more (efficient/engaging/_____) for new customers?

3. Can we develop a more systematic approach to (collecting/acting/_____) on customer feedback post-purchase?

4. What has been the impact of our follow-up efforts on customer retention and loyalty, based on recent (data/feedback/_____)?

5. How can we better collaborate across (departments/offices/_____) to ensure a seamless post-sale experience for our customers?

(5) Salesperson to External Stakeholders or Partners:

1. How can we work together to enhance the post-sale experience for customers, particularly in terms of (support/onboarding/_____)?

2. What (tools/resources/_____) can you provide to help us better support our customers after their purchase?

3. Can you share (insights/strategies/_____) from your experience that has effectively increased customer loyalty post-sale?

4. How does our collaboration after the sale benefit our customers and make our offerings more valuable?

5. What feedback have you received from customers about their post-purchase experience, and how can we use this to improve our follow-up process?

B.   ASKING FOR REFERRALS:

For you aiming to expand you network through referrals, these questions are key. They guide you in engaging satisfied clients to advocate for your product or service, thus fostering new business opportunities. By inquiring about potential referrals, discussing the benefits of sharing your solution with others, and understanding the best ways to facilitate this exchange, you reinforce the value of your offering and encourage clients to introduce your brand to their circles, driving growth.

(1) Salesperson to Client:

1. After seeing the benefits of our (product/service/_____), do you know anyone else who could benefit from what we offer?

2. We're grateful for your feedback on our (solution/service/_____). Could you refer us to others who might have similar needs?

3. Who comes to mind that could also benefit from the (cost savings/efficiency/_____) you've experienced with our (product/service/_____)?

4. Given your positive experience, would you be comfortable sharing our contact with (colleagues/friends/_____) who needs our (products/services/_____)?

5. Can we count on you to spread the word about how our (product/service/_____) has helped you achieve your (goals/objectives/_____)?

6. Would you be willing to introduce us to (one/two/_____) business contacts who might benefit from a similar (solution/service/_____)?

7. How can we make it easier for you to share your success story with our (product/service/_____) with your network?

8. Are there any (events/networking opportunities/_____) where you think our solutions could interest others in your industry?

9. What incentives would encourage you to refer our (products/services/_____) to your peers?

10. Would you be open to taking part in a case study that we can share with potential clients, possibly encouraging (referrals/business opportunities/_____)?

(2) Client to Salesperson:

1. How have others successfully referred your (products/services/_____) to their network?

2. Can you provide me with some (information/materials/_____) that I can share with potential referrals?

3. What benefits might my referrals receive for considering your (product/service/_____)?

4. Are there any referral (incentives/programs/_____) currently available for both the referrer and referee?

5. How can I ensure that my contacts will receive the same level of (service/attention/_____) that I did?

6. What success stories can you share where referrals have significantly benefited from your (solutions/offerings/_____)?

7. How do you track and acknowledge referrals I make to ensure (recognition/rewards/_____) are accurately distributed?

8. What is the process for my referrals to access special (offers/deals/_____) when they mention my name or company?

9. Can you detail how your referral process works to make it easy for me to refer your (product/service/_____)?

10. What support do you offer to first-time clients referred by me to ensure their (onboarding/experience/_____) is seamless?

(3) Salesperson to Self:

1. Have I clearly communicated the value of referring new clients to my (existing customers/former clients/_____)?

2. What strategies can I implement to remind clients of the referral program without being intrusive?

3. How can I better express (gratitude/disappointment/_____) for referrals, regardless of their immediate outcome?

4. What timing has proven most effective for asking for referrals, and how can I incorporate this into my follow-up process?

5. How can I personalize referral requests to make each client feel (valued/understood/_____)?

(4) Salesperson to Colleagues/Internal Team:

1. What has been your most effective approach in asking for and receiving referrals?

2. Can we brainstorm (incentives/rewards/_____) that encourage clients to refer their contacts to us?

3. How do we (track/reward/_____) successful referrals to ensure we're (recognizing/thanking/_____) our clients appropriately?

4. What feedback have we received from clients about our referral process, and how can we use this to improve?

5. How can we better (integrate/foster/_____) referral requests into our post-sale engagement strategy to make it a seamless part of our interaction?

(5) Salesperson to External Stakeholders or Partners:

1. How can we collaborate to create a mutually beneficial referral program that leverages both our networks?

2. Have you seen any successful referral (strategies/approach/_____) in your network that we could adapt for our use?

3. Can you provide examples of incentives that have effectively motivated your (clients/partners/_____) to make referrals?

4. What (tools/platforms/_____) do you recommend for (managing/tracking/_____) referrals to ensure proper acknowledgment and rewards?

5. How can we work together to maximize the potential of referrals, possibly through (joint marketing efforts/co-hosted events/_____)?

C.   ADDITIONAL CONSIDERATIONS:

Post-sale engagement is crucial for deepening customer relationships and encouraging loyalty. It involves strategies to introduce customers to additional products, involve them in loyalty programs, and engage them in user communities. Effective post-sale communication can uncover opportunities for upselling, enhance customer experiences, and gather valuable feedback for future improvements. This phase is essential for maintaining relevance to customers' needs and fostering a long-lasting partnership that goes beyond the initial transaction.

(1) Salesperson to Client:

1. Based on your current use of our (product/service/_____), have you considered exploring our other solutions that could (enhance/optimize/_____) your experience?

2. Are you aware of our loyalty program that rewards clients for (repeat purchases/referrals/_____), and would you be interested in learning more?

3. We have a community of users where clients share (tips/experiences/_____). Would you be interested in joining to get more out of your (product/service/_____)?

4. Can we personalize our communications to you based on your interests, such as (new product launches/special offers/_____)?

5. How can we assist you in discovering additional products that complement your recent purchase, such as (accessories/upgrades/_____)?

6. Would you be interested in receiving personalized recommendations based on your purchase (history/feedback/_____)?

7. Have you explored all the features of your current product, and can we assist with any (training/onboarding/_____)?

8. Are there any specific (challenges/needs/_____) you're facing that our other solutions might address?

9. Would a (discount/reward/_____) for your next purchase or for referring others encourage you to explore more of our offerings?

10. How do you prefer to receive updates and offers from us, ensuring they add value to your (business/daily use/_____)?

(2) Client to Salesperson:

1. What other (products/services/_____) do you offer that could complement my current setup?

2. Can you explain the benefits of joining your loyalty program and how it works?

3. How can I connect with other users to learn more about optimizing my use of your product?

4. Are there any upcoming (promotions/new product launches/_____) that might be relevant to my interests?

5. How do you tailor (recommendations/communications/_____) to individual clients?

6. Can you show me how to introduce your (services/products/_____) to my network effectively?

7. What specific advantages will my contacts gain by using your (solution/technology/_____) based on my recommendation?

8. Are there special (offers/discounts/_____) available for clients I refer to your company?

9. How do you ensure high-quality service for the people I refer to your (business/brand/_____)?

10. Can you give examples of successful referrals that led to significant (benefits/savings/_____) for both the referrer and the referred?

(3) Salesperson to Self:

1. Have I fully (explored/understood/_____) the client's needs to identify opportunities for (cross-selling/upselling/_____) effectively?

2. Am I adequately informed about all our (products/services/_____) to make relevant recommendations?

3. How can I improve my approach to introducing clients to our (loyalty programs/community forums/_____)?

4. In what ways can I personalize my communication with clients to ensure higher (engagement/satisfaction/_____)?

5. What feedback have I received from clients that can help me refine my post-sale engagement strategy?

(4) Salesperson to Colleagues/Internal Team:

1. What strategies have been effective in (cross-selling/upselling/_____) to existing clients?

2. How can we better promote our loyalty program to encourage repeat business and deepen client engagement?

3. Can we collaborate to create more engaging content for our community forums that encourages participation?

4. What insights have we gained from (personalized communications/failed cross-selling efforts/_____) that led to increased client satisfaction and sales?

5. How can we leverage client feedback to improve our (product offerings/post-sale engagement practices/_____)?

(5) Salesperson to External Stakeholders or Partners:

1. How can we collaborate to offer (bundled solutions/promotions/_____) that benefit our mutual clients?

2. What have you learned from your loyalty programs that could help us enhance ours?

3. Can you share successful strategies for (building/maintaining/_____) active (online communities/recurring clients/_____)?

4. How do you personalize communication with your clients, and what tools do you use to achieve this?

5. What feedback mechanisms have you found most effective in (gathering/acting/_____) on client insights?

11. FOSTERING CUSTOMER ADVOCACY AND LOYALTY

A. CREATING ADVOCATES:

This collection of questions is crafted to transform satisfied customers into active brand advocates. By encouraging the sharing of success stories, feedback, and participation in advocacy programs, these queries support you in nurturing loyalty, enhancing brand visibility, and building deeper customer connections. Suitable for various interactions—from direct client engagement to internal team collaboration and external partnerships—these questions are pivotal in fostering a community of supporters at every stage of the customer journey.

(1) Salesperson to Client:

1. How has our (product/service/_____) made a positive impact on your (business/daily routine/_____)?

2. Would you be willing to share your success story with our (product/service/_____) through a (testimonial/case study/_____)?

3. Can we feature your (review/story/_____) on our social media platforms to inspire others?

4. How can we make it easier for you to refer our (product/service/_____) to your (colleagues/friends/_____)?

5. Would you be interested in participating in a customer spotlight feature, showcasing how you've utilized our (product/service/_____) to achieve your goals?

6. Are there any specific aspects of our (service/product/_____) you think would benefit others in your (industry/network/_____)?

7. How likely are you to recommend our (product/service/_____) to others based on your experience?

8. What incentives could encourage you to share your experiences with our (products/services/_____) more broadly?

9. Would you be open to creating (user-generated content/reviews/_____) that we could share to help others understand the value of our offerings?

10. Can we send you a personalized thank-you (message/gift/_____) to show our appreciation for your support and feedback?

(2) Client to Salesperson:

1. How can I provide feedback that might help improve your (products/services/_____)?

2. Are there any platforms or forums where I can share my positive experiences with your (product/service/_____)?

3. What kind of (rewards/incentives/_____) do you offer for referrals or for sharing testimonials?

4. How can I get involved in your community or customer advocacy programs?

5. Can you guide me on how to create engaging content that highlights my experience with your (product/service/_____)?

(3) Salesperson to Self:

1. Have I effectively communicated the value of becoming a brand advocate to my clients?

2. What strategies can I employ to personalize my appreciation for customers' referrals and content sharing?

3. How can I better identify customers who are most likely to become brand advocates based on their satisfaction and engagement levels?

4. What additional (tools/resources/_____) can I leverage to encourage and simplify the process of creating user-generated content for our clients?

5. How can I ensure that every customer feels valued and appreciated, increasing their likelihood of becoming a loyal advocate?

(4) Salesperson to Colleagues/Internal Team:

1. What has been the most effective method for encouraging satisfied customers to share their stories or refer our (products/services/_____)?

2. How can we better showcase customer success stories and testimonials to build trust with potential clients?

3. What feedback have we received from our advocacy or loyalty programs, and how can we use this to improve?

4. Can we brainstorm new incentives for referrals and user-generated content that align with our brand values?

5. How can we personalize our thank-you messages or gifts to make them more impactful and memorable for our customers?

(5) Salesperson to External Stakeholders or Partners:

1. How can we collaborate to create more compelling customer advocacy initiatives that benefit both our brands?

2. Can you share examples of successful (referral programs/loyalty programs/_____) from your experience that we could adapt?

3. What (tools/platforms/_____) do you recommend for tracking and rewarding customer referrals and advocacy effectively?

4. How can we integrate our products or services more seamlessly to encourage cross-promotion and referrals between our customer bases?

5. What strategies have you found effective in turning satisfied customers into vocal brand advocates, especially in a digital context?

B. LOYALTY PROGRAMS AND ENGAGEMENT:

Fostering customer advocacy and loyalty is key to sustained business growth. After a sale, engaging clients to share their positive experiences can transform them into brand advocates. This involves assessing their satisfaction, encouraging story sharing, leveraging social media, facilitating referrals, and recognizing their contributions. A strategic approach to post-sale engagement not only enhances client relationships but also amplifies your brand's reach and reputation through genuine, customer-driven advocacy.

(1) Salesperson to Client:

1. How can we design our loyalty program to align with your (values/needs/_____) and ensure it delivers (value/relevance/_____) to you?

2. What (rewards/benefits/_____) would motivate you to take part more actively in our loyalty program?

3. Have you had the chance to use any of our (exclusive previews/special access/_____), and how can we make these opportunities more appealing?

4. In what ways can we improve our loyalty program to better (recognize/reward/_____) your continued business?

5. Would you prefer a loyalty program that offers (tiered rewards/points for purchases/_____), and why?

6. How often would you like to receive (feedback requests/updates/_____) from us regarding new offers or products?

7. What exclusive (content/events/_____) would you find most valuable as part of our loyalty program?

8. Are there specific types of user-generated content you would be more inclined to (create/share/_____) as part of our loyalty incentives?

9. How can we make our loyalty program more (engaging/easier/_____) for you to take part in?

10. Would you be interested in a referral bonus as part of our loyalty program, and what would make this appealing to you?

(2) Client to Salesperson:

1. What are the different (levels/tiers/_____) in your loyalty program, and how can I advance to the next level?

2. Can you provide examples of how customers have (benefited/enjoyed/_____) from your loyalty program in the past?

3. What kinds of exclusive (access/previews/_____) do loyal customers get, and how often do these opportunities arise?

4. How are rewards in your loyalty program tailored to match customer (preferences/purchase history/_____)?

5. How can I track my (points/rewards/_____) accumulation and see what rewards I'm eligible for?

6. Are there any (partnerships/collaborations/_____) that enhance the value of your loyalty program through external (offers/discounts/_____)?

7. What (actions/activities/_____) contribute to earning points faster in the loyalty program?

8. How does the loyalty program integrate with your (app/website/_____), making it easier for me to manage my benefits?

9. What measures are in place to ensure the (privacy/security/_____) of my loyalty program data?

10. In the event of a (problem/dispute/_____) regarding the loyalty program, what is the (process/contact method/_____) for resolution?

(3) Salesperson to Self:

1. Have I fully understood the (preferences/needs/_____) of my clients to offer them a loyalty program that truly engages them?

2. How can I better communicate the (benefits/opportunities/_____) of our loyalty program to encourage participation?

3. What adjustments can I make to ensure our loyalty program is (competitive/appealing/_____) compared to others in the market?

4. How effectively am I using customer feedback to continually enhance our loyalty program?

5. What new strategies can I implement to increase participation in our loyalty program and turn customers into advocates?

(4) Salesperson to Colleagues/Internal Team:

1. What approaches have proven effective in tailoring our loyalty program to (different customer segments/personal preferences/_____)?

2. How can we improve interdepartmental collaboration to efficiently collect and implement (customer feedback/suggestions/_____)?

3. What innovative (rewards/incentives/_____) have we not yet explored that could enhance our loyalty program?

4. Can we share success stories of customer engagement through our loyalty program to (inspire new ideas/engage new customers/_____)?

5. How can we leverage (technology/former customers/_____) to personalize our loyalty program offerings and communications more effectively?

(5) Salesperson to External Stakeholders or Partners:

1. How can we collaborate to enhance our loyalty program by offering (joint rewards/benefits/_____)?

2. What insights from your loyalty program experience can guide us in refining our offerings to (increase engagement/maximize value/_____)?

3. How can we leverage cross-promotion to enrich our loyalty programs with (unique experiences/special offers/_____)?

4. In what ways can your (platforms/services/_____) help us collect and act on customer feedback to improve our loyalty program?

5. Can you share strategies or tools that enable the delivery of (exclusive content/personalized rewards/_____) to enhance engagement in our loyalty program?

C.   ADDITIONAL CONSIDERATIONS:

Building customer advocacy and loyalty is crucial in establishing a lasting relationship beyond the initial sale. These questions are designed to guide sales professionals in engaging customers effectively post-purchase. By focusing on creating a valued community, personalizing communications, and recognizing customer contributions, you can enhance loyalty and transform customers into brand advocates. This approach is essential for nurturing a supportive ecosystem where customers feel appreciated and motivated to share their positive experiences.

(1) Salesperson to Client:

1. Would you be interested in joining our online community to connect with other (users/customers/_____) and share your experiences?

2. How can we personalize our (online community/communications/_____) to better meet your interests, such as offering (tailored advice/special discounts/_____)?

3. Have you had the opportunity to take advantage of our customer success program to optimize your use of our (product/service/_____)?

4. What incentives can we offer that would encourage you to share your feedback about our (products/services/_____) more frequently?

5. How would you like to be recognized for your contributions to our (community/blog/_____) or for providing valuable feedback?

6. Are there specific types of (content/events/_____) you would like to see more of in our (community forums/social media groups/_____)?

7. Can we provide you with (exclusive access/early previews/_____) to new (products/services/_____) based on your loyalty level?

8. What type of personalized communication do you find most valuable when learning about (product updates/upcoming events/_____)?

9. Would you be interested in a loyalty program that offers (tiered rewards/points for feedback/_____), and what would make it appealing to you?

10. How can we better support your success with our (product/service/_____) through our customer success programs?

(2) Client to Salesperson:

1. How can I get involved in your (loyalty program/rewards program/_____), and what are the benefits for participating?

2. What kind of personalized (offers/content/_____) do you provide, and how are they tailored to individual customer preferences?

3. Can you tell me more about how to contribute to your user-generated content initiatives and what incentives are available?

4. How does your customer success program work, and how can it help me achieve better results with your (product/service/_____)?

5. Are there opportunities for customers like me to provide (input/feedback/_____) that directly influences product development or service improvements?

6. How can I take part in your (customer advocacy/community engagement/_____) efforts to share my positive experience with others?

7. What (channels/platforms/_____) do you recommend for sharing my (testimonials/reviews/_____) of your (products/services/_____)?

8. How are (feedback/suggestions/_____) from customers like me used to enhance your (product line/service offerings/_____)?

9. Are there specific (guidelines/templates/_____) for creating user-generated content that aligns with your brand's messaging?

10. How can I learn about (upcoming events/webinars/_____) that focus on maximizing the benefits of your (products/services/_____)?

(3) Salesperson to Self:

1. Have I effectively communicated the (value/extra features/_____) of our community-building efforts to customers?

2. What strategies can I employ to enhance personalization in our communications, ensuring each customer feels uniquely valued?

3. How can I more proactively identify opportunities for customers to engage with our (customer success programs/loyalty program/_____)?

4. What feedback have I received that can help refine our approach to rewarding (customer feedback/customer participation/_____)?

5. How can I ensure that our (loyalty programs/engagement strategies/_____) are continuously evolving to meet the changing (needs/preferences/_____) of our customers?

(4) Salesperson to Colleagues/Internal Team:

1. How can we collaborate to create (more engaging/valuable/_____) content for our online communities?

2. What best practices have we identified for (segmenting/personalizing/_____) our loyalty program offerings?

3. Can we share insights on the most effective ways to collect and act on (customer feedback/complaints/_____)?

4. What new (technologies/tools/_____) can we leverage to enhance our personalization efforts at scale?

5. How can we better integrate customer success programs into our overall (strategy/marketing plans/_____) to ensure customer advocacy and loyalty?

(5) Salesperson to External Stakeholders or Partners:

1. How can we work together to offer exclusive (benefits/content/_____) to our loyal customers and community members?

2. What insights can you share from your experience with personalizing customer engagement at scale?

3. Are there partnership opportunities that could enhance our loyalty programs or customer success initiatives?

4. How can we collaborate on (gathering/rewarding/_____) customer feedback in a way that benefits both our organizations?

5. Can you provide examples of successful (community-building strategies/new loyalty programs/_____) that have fostered customer advocacy and loyalty in your network?

12. CONTINUOUS IMPROVEMENT AND PERSONAL DEVELOPMENT

A.   SKILL DEVELOPMENT:

These questions aim to guide you in identifying areas for skill enhancement, embracing continuous learning, and fostering a culture of resilience and adaptability. Suitable for engaging with clients, internal teams, and external partners, they encourage a proactive approach to professional development, ensuring sales strategies remain innovative and aligned with evolving market demands and client needs.

(1) Salesperson to Client:

1. What specific areas of (training/support/_____) would you find most beneficial for maximizing the value of our (solutions/services/_____)?

2. Could you identify any (services/products/_____) gaps you perceive in our offerings that, if filled, would significantly benefit your organization?

3. In what areas do you feel our sales team could improve our (knowledge/skills/_____) to better support your (objectives/needs/_____)?

4. Are there specific (training sessions/product demonstrations/_____) we can provide to ensure you're fully leveraging our (solutions/technology/_____)?

5. How can we enhance our sales approach to better align with your strategic goals, particularly in (market insights/product customization/_____)?

6. What type of feedback do you have on (our communication style/the effectiveness of our sales presentations/_____) in meeting your expectations?

7. Would you find value in more specialized sales support focused on your industry's specific challenges and how our (products/services/_____) can address them?

8. Are there areas of our (product/service/_____) training that you think need enhancement to improve your user experience or outcome?

9. Would you be open to participating in a feedback session aimed at improving our sales team's understanding of your (sector's challenges/preferred solutions/_____)?

10. How can our sales team better facilitate your decision-making process through improved knowledge in (competitive analysis/ROI calculations/_____)?

(2) Client to Salesperson:

1. Can you detail the (training/specialization/_____) your sales team undergoes to stay informed about (industry trends/product advancements/_____)?

2. How does your sales team incorporate (customer feedback/peer learning/_____) into their continuous improvement process?

3. What measures do you take to ensure your sales representatives have in-depth knowledge of (specific markets/technical aspects/_____)?

4. How do you assess and enhance your sales team's skills in (communication/negotiation/_____) to better meet client needs?

5. Could you explain how ongoing (education/training programs/_____) are personalized for each salesperson's development needs?

6. What opportunities do your salespeople have for (peer learning/collaboration/_____) with experts within your industry?

7. How frequently does your sales team receive (updates/training/_____) on new (products/services/_____) to ensure they are well-informed?

8. In what ways do you encourage your sales staff to (self-assess/seek feedback/_____) for personal and professional growth?

9. Can you share examples of how your sales team has (adapted/evolved/_____) in response to changing market demands or client feedback?

10. How does your organization support salespeople in developing (specialized skills/industry expertise/_____) to offer more value to clients?

(3) Salesperson to Self:

1. What areas of my sales (technique/knowledge/_____) require improvement, and what actions can I take to develop those (technique/knowledge/_____)?

2. How can I enhance my (product knowledge/industry expertise(technique/knowledge/_____) to provide more value to my clients?

3. In what ways can I (engage in peer learning/find a mentor/_____) within the industry to enhance my sales capabilities?

4. What steps can I take to specialize in a certain area of (sales/cold calling/_____), and how will this specialization benefit my clients?

5. How can I better collect and act on feedback from clients to continuously improve my (sales approach/elevator speech/_____)?

(4) Salesperson to Colleagues/Internal Team:

1. Can we share (insights/strategies/_____) on how to engage effectively in (peer learning/mentoring within our team/_____)?

2. What (resources/training opportunities/_____) have you found beneficial for staying ahead in our industry and enhancing sales skills?

3. How can we collaborate to create a more specialized approach in our sales techniques for different segments of our customer base?

4. What mechanisms do we have in place for (collecting/using/_____) customer feedback to improve our sales process?

5. How can we support each other in pursuing continuous (education/specialization/_____) in our sales roles?

(5) Salesperson to External Stakeholders or Partners:

1. How can we collaborate to make sure our sales teams have the most up-to-date (product knowledge/industry insights/_____)?

2. What opportunities exist for our sales team to learn from your expertise and vice versa?

3. Are there joint (training/development/_____) programs we can engage in to enhance our (sales effectiveness/market understanding/_____)?

4. How can your organization help us in developing a more specialized sales approach tailored to our (shared/unique/_____) market segments?

5. Can we establish a feedback loop between our organizations to share insights on customer needs and preferences, improving our sales strategies?

B.   GOAL SETTING:

These questions guide you through establishing and reaching your goals, emphasizing SMART criteria for effective goal setting. Tailored for self-assessment, client engagement, team alignment, and partner collaboration, they promote discussions on realistic target setting, progress monitoring, flexibility, and leveraging support for continuous growth. Use these prompts to foster a structured approach to achieving sales objectives and advancing personal and professional development.

(1) Salesperson to Client:

1. How do you envision your (business objectives/career milestones/_____) evolving over the next (year/5 years/_____)?

2. Can you identify specific (short-term/long-term/_____) goals that our (products/services/_____) could help you achieve?

3. What are the most critical (milestones/targets/_____) you aim to reach in the upcoming (quarter/year/_____)?

4. How do you prioritize your goals to ensure they are both (achievable/relevant/_____) to your overarching strategy?

5. What challenges have you faced in setting and achieving your (personal/business/_____) goals in the past?

6. In what ways can we assist in defining clearer (performance indicators/success metrics/_____) for your goals?

7. How do you measure progress towards your (short-term/long-term/_____) objectives, and how can we support this process?

8. Could you share how aligning your goals with our (solutions/strategies/_____) has impacted your achievement rate?

9. What specific (tools/resources/_____) do you need to effectively track and meet your targeted goals?

10. How often do you review and adjust your goals to ensure they remain (relevant/attainable/_____) in a changing environment?

(2) Client to Salesperson:

1. How can your (products/services/_____) help me achieve my specific (sales targets/business goals/_____) within the next (quarter/year/_____)?

2. Can you provide examples of how other clients have set and achieved their (short-term/long-term/_____) goals using your solutions?

3. What strategies do you recommend for setting realistic yet challenging (sales/productivity/_____) goals in my industry?

4. How does your company support goal tracking and measurement, particularly for (new product launches/customer acquisition/_____)?

5. What (tools/resources/_____) do you offer to help clients like me monitor progress towards our defined goals?

6. How adaptable are your (services/products/_____) to changing (goals/market conditions/_____)?

7. Can you guide me on setting (SMART/attainable/_____) goals that align with the capabilities of your (product/service/_____)?

8. What role does customer feedback play in your process of helping clients set and achieve their goals?

9. Are there any case studies or testimonials that highlight the effectiveness of your (products/services/_____) in goal attainment?

10. How do you ensure that the goals we set together are not only achievable but also sustainable and aligned with my long-term (business strategy/career development/_____)?

(3) Salesperson to Self:

1. Have I clearly defined my (sales targets/personal development goals/) for this (quarter/year/), ensuring they are SMART?

2. How do my current goals align with the broader objectives of my (team/organization/_____) and how can I better synchronize them?

3. What specific (skills/knowledge areas/_____) do I need to develop to achieve my short-term and long-term goals effectively?

4. In what areas have I consistently fallen short, and what new strategies can I implement to address these gaps?

5. How am I tracking my progress towards these goals, and do I need to adjust my (tracking methods/tools/_____) for better clarity?

(4) Salesperson to Colleagues/Internal Team:

1. How do our individual goals align with the team's overall (objectives/goals/_____), and where can we find opportunities for synergy or collaboration?

2. What specific (sales techniques/learning resources/_____) have you found most effective in reaching your sales targets?

3. Can we share insights on setting realistic yet challenging (quarterly/annual/_____) sales goals based on (market trends/past performance/_____)?

4. How do you incorporate feedback from (clients/management/_____) into your goal-setting process to ensure continuous improvement?

5. In what ways can we support each other in achieving our (personal/team/_____) goals, especially in areas where we face common challenges?

(5) Salesperson to External Stakeholders or Partners:

1. How can our partnership goals be aligned to support mutual growth and achievement of (sales targets/strategic objectives/_____)?

2. Can you share successful strategies from your experience in setting and achieving (market expansion/customer acquisition/_____) goals?

3. In what ways can we leverage each other's strengths to set more effective joint (marketing/sales/_____) goals?

4. How often should we review and adjust our collaborative goals to ensure they remain (relevant/achievable/_____) amidst market changes?

5. How do you suggest we address potential challenges or obstacles in achieving our (partnership/project/_____) goals?

C.   TIME MANAGEMENT:

These questions are designed to enhance your time management skills within the sales process, aiding you in prioritizing tasks, leveraging efficient tools and techniques, and ensuring productive delegation and necessary downtime. Suitable for discussions between you and clients, within teams, and for self-reflection, they aim to optimize daily activities, reduce burnout, and improve overall efficiency and productivity in achieving sales goals and maintaining a high level of client service.

(1) Salesperson to Client:

1. How can we help streamline your procurement process to save you time when ordering our (products/services/_____)?

2. What are your primary challenges in managing time effectively for implementing new (solutions/technologies/_____)?

3. Can we offer training sessions that fit within your busy schedule to ensure you're getting the most out of our (product/service/_____) efficiently?

4. Can you identify specific tasks related to our (product/service/_____) that you believe could be automated or simplified to improve your team's time management?

5. How do you currently prioritize your needs when deciding to invest in new (tools/resources/_____), and how can we assist in that decision-making process?

6. What features would you like to see in our (product/service/_____) that could help you manage your time more effectively?

7. How often would you prefer (check-ins/updates/_____) from us to ensure efficient use of your time while staying informed about our (offerings/updates/_____)?

8. Can we provide any (templates/guides/_____) to help you more quickly integrate our (product/service/_____) into your workflow?

9. Would you find a (personalized dashboard/reporting tool/_____) useful for monitoring the impact of our (product/service/_____) on your time management and productivity?

10. How do you allocate time for evaluating and reflecting on the effectiveness of new (strategies/tools/_____) like ours in achieving your business objectives?

(2) Client to Salesperson:

1. What is the speed at which you can implement your (product/service/_____) into our existing systems without significant downtime?

2. Can you offer any (tips/best practices/_____) for managing our time more effectively when using your (software/tools/_____)?

3. Are there any features in your (product/service/_____) specifically designed to help users save time on (daily tasks/project management/_____)?

4. How does your (customer support/training program/_____) work to ensure we're not wasting time figuring out how to use the (product/service/_____)?

5. What kind of (automation/integration/_____) options does your solution offer to help streamline our operations?

6. Can you provide a timeline for seeing tangible time-saving results after implementing your (product/service/_____)?

7. How do you prioritize (updates/new features/_____) to ensure minimal disruption to our workflow and time management?

8. Do you have any (case studies/examples/_____) where your (product/service/_____) significantly improved time management for a client in our industry?

9. What measures do you take to ensure the onboarding process for your (product/service/_____) is as time efficient as possible?

10. How flexible are your (training sessions/implementation plans/_____) to accommodate our team's busy schedule?

(3) Salesperson to Self:

1. How can I better prioritize my tasks to ensure I'm focusing on activities that directly contribute to my (sales goals/client satisfaction/_____)?

2. What strategies can I implement to improve my efficiency in handling (client communications/sales paperwork/_____), freeing up more time for high-value activities?

3. In what areas could I benefit from delegating tasks or seeking support to manage my workload more effectively and focus on (closing deals/building relationships/_____)?

4. How can I ensure that I'm allocating enough time to continuously improve my sales techniques and strategies through (self-reflection/professional development/_____)?

5. What changes can I make to my daily routine to incorporate downtime and prevent burnout, ensuring I maintain a high level of productivity and (engagement/motivation/_____)?

(4) Salesperson to Colleagues/Internal Team:

1. How do you effectively manage your time to balance between (client meetings/sales tasks/_____) and personal development activities?

2. Can you share any (tools/techniques/_____) that have helped you improve efficiency in (tracking leads/following up with clients/_____)?

3. In our team's experience, what tasks have been most effectively delegated to support staff or automated to free up more time for (sales-focused activities/strategy development/_____)?

4. How do you incorporate (reflection/learning/_____) into your busy schedule to ensure continuous improvement in your sales approach?

5. What strategies have you found most effective in ensuring downtime is taken regularly to prevent burnout and maintain (productivity/creativity/_____)?

(5) Salesperson to External Stakeholders or Partners:

1. How have you successfully integrated (time management tools/partner technologies/_____) to streamline (communication/collaboration/_____) between our teams?

2. Can you share examples of (efficiency improvements/process optimizations/_____) achieved through our partnership that have significantly saved time for your sales teams?

3. In what ways can we leverage our partnership to further reduce the time spent on (administrative tasks/client management/_____) and focus more on sales and relationship building?

4. What strategies do you recommend for effectively managing our joint projects to ensure timely delivery and maximum (productivity/efficiency/_____)?

5. How can we better align our (planning/scheduling/_____) practices to optimize the time spent on collaborative initiatives and enhance the overall outcome for both parties?

D.   ADDITIONAL CONSIDERATIONS:

These questions are designed to guide you towards enhancing your emotional intelligence, networking skills, adaptability, and overall well-being. Suitable for various stages of the sales process, they aim to improve client interactions, foster internal collaboration, and build stronger external partnerships. By focusing on these key areas, you can achieve both personal and professional growth, ensuring you are equipped to navigate the complexities of the sales landscape effectively.

(1) Salesperson to Client:

1. How can we adapt our services to better support your professional development and (networking opportunities/industry engagement/_____)?

2. In what ways can our partnership contribute to your team's (emotional intelligence/adaptability/_____) in navigating industry changes?

3. Are there specific (training programs/workshops/_____) you'd like us to provide that focus on personal development and industry trends?

4. How important is it for you to have access to resources that enhance (well-being/professional growth/_____) within your organization?

5. Can we organize (discussions/networking events/_____) that promote sharing of best practices and ongoing improvement among professionals in your industry?

6. What role do you see (mental health support/professional coaching/_____) playing in your team's performance and satisfaction?

7. How can our (products/services/_____) be tailored to better meet the needs of your team's ongoing (education/development/_____)?

8. Would you be interested in collaborations that offer insights into (emerging technologies/industry shifts/_____), fostering a culture of (adaptability/innovation/_____)?

9. What strategies have you found effective for maintaining (work-life balance/personal well-being/_____) while pursuing career goals?

10. How can we help create a more (engaging/empowering/_____) work environment that supports both personal and professional development for your team?

(2) Client to Salesperson:

1. What initiatives does your company have in place to support (continuous learning/emotional intelligence/_____) in our team?

2. How do you ensure your sales team remains (adaptable/resilient/_____) in the face of industry (changes/ challenges/_____)?

3. Can you provide (training/resources/_____) that helps us enhance our team's (professional development/industry engagement/_____)?

4. In what ways can your services help us foster a culture of (well-being/growth mindset/_____) within our organization?

5. How does your company prioritize (networking opportunities/professional development/_____) for clients like us?

6. Are there any programs or partnerships you offer that focus on improving (personal effectiveness/team dynamics/_____)?

7. How do you tailor your solutions to support clients in achieving their (personal development/career advancement/_____) goals?

8. What support can we expect from you in implementing strategies that encourage (emotional intelligence/adaptability/_____) among our staff?

9. How can your (products/services/_____) facilitate our engagement with the latest (industry trends/technological advancements/_____)?

10. What measures do you take to ensure the (health/well-being/_____) of your clients through your (services/products/_____)?

(3) Salesperson to Self:

1. How can I actively improve my (emotional intelligence/relationship-building skills/_____) to foster better connections with (clients/colleagues/_____)?

2. In what areas do I need to be more (adaptable/resilient/_____), and how can I develop these qualities?

3. What actions will I take to expand my (network/professional relationships/_____) within and outside my industry?

4. What measures can I take to ensure I'm maintaining a (healthy/work-life balance/_____) while striving for sales excellence?

5. What steps can I take to foster a mindset of (growth/continuous learning/_____) in every aspect of my sales career?

(4) Salesperson to Colleagues/Internal Team:

1. How can we collectively enhance our (emotional intelligence/team dynamics/_____) to improve our (collaboration/client relationships/_____)?

2. In what ways can we support each other in becoming more (adaptable/resilient/_____) to changes within our industry and sales processes?

3. How can we more effectively leverage our internal (networks/knowledge/_____) to facilitate each other's professional growth?

4. What feedback mechanisms can we implement to ensure we're all contributing to and benefiting from continuous (improvement/learning/_____)?

5. Are there opportunities for us to develop a shared resource or tool that enhances our (skillsets/professional development/_____)?

(5) Salesperson to External Stakeholders or Partners:

1. How can our collaboration support mutual growth in (emotional intelligence/industry knowledge/_____), benefiting both our teams and clients?

2. What initiatives could we co-create to enhance (networking opportunities/professional development/_____) within our respective industries?

3. How can we leverage our partnership to gain insights and (training/mentorship/_____) from each other's (expertise/networks/_____)?

4. Can you suggest tools or resources that have been effective in promoting (skill development/emotional intelligence/_____) within your organization?

5. How can we create a feedback loop between our organizations that enhances both our (sales effectiveness/client relationships/_____) and contributes to our teams' development?

13. MEASURING THE IMPACT OF SALES NARRATIVES

A.   FEEDBACK LOOPS FOR STORY REFINEMENT:

These questions aim to enhance sales narratives by incorporating feedback from various interactions. They're intended to refine your approach, ensuring your stories resonate with clients and stand out from the competition. By fostering open dialogue for feedback and self-assessment, these questions help identify improvements, making narratives more impactful. Ideal after presentations or in follow-up meetings, they support ongoing development and alignment with client expectations and market trends.

(1) Salesperson to Client:

1. How did our sales story resonate with you to address your (needs/pain points/_____)?

2. Can you give us specific feedback on how to (improve/transform/_____) our narrative so that it better aligns with your (business goals/personal needs/_____)?

3. Did our sales presentation clearly articulate the value proposition of our (product/service/_____)?

4. Were there elements of our story that (particularly captured your interest/seemed irrelevant to your situation/_____)?

5. How effectively do you feel our sales narrative differentiated our (product/service/_____) from competitors?

6. Is there (additional information/a different focus/_____) you would have preferred to see in our sales narrative?

7. How compelling was our story in motivating you to take action or consider our (product/service/_____)?

8. Would you suggest any changes to our approach that might make our narrative more compelling to others in your industry?

9. Did our sales narrative help clarify how our (solution/service/_____) could solve your specific challenges?

10. How can we better tailor our sales narratives in the future to align with (your expectations/industry standards/_____)?

(2) Client to Salesperson:

1. How do you measure the effectiveness of your sales narratives in engaging (clients/prospects/_____)?

2. Can you share examples of how (client/customer/_____) feedback has shaped the evolution of your sales stories?

3. What mechanisms do you have in place to gather (feedback/insights/_____) on your sales presentations from other clients?

4. How often do you (review/update/_____) your sales narratives based on (customer insights/client feedback/_____)?

5. What impact have you seen on (sales outcomes/client engagement/_____) from refining your stories with client feedback?

6. How do you ensure that the stories you tell resonate with a (diverse client base/specific audience/_____)?

7. Can you describe a specific instance where (feedback/insights/_____) significantly changed your sales approach?

8. What strategies do you employ to encourage (honest feedback/constructive criticism/_____) from clients on your sales narratives?

9. How do you balance maintaining your core sales message with adapting to (individual client feedback/market trends/_____)?

10. In what ways have you noticed changes in (client engagement/customer satisfaction/_____) after refining your narratives based on feedback?

(3) Salesperson to Self:

1. What specific (changes/improvements/_____) have I made to my stories based on feedback, and how have they impacted my sales results?

2. Am I actively seeking (constructive criticism/insights/_____) from clients to improve my storytelling techniques?

3. How do I measure the success of my adjusted sales narratives in terms of (engagement rates/close rates/_____)?

4. In what areas of my sales presentation can I better incorporate client (experiences/stories/_____) to make my pitch more compelling?

5. How can I better document and analyze the (feedback/responses/_____) from clients about my sales stories for ongoing improvement?

(4) Salesperson to Colleagues/Internal Team:

1. How have you successfully incorporated (client feedback/industry trends/_____) into your sales stories to improve their impact?

2. How do we measure the effectiveness of our revised sales narratives in achieving (higher engagement/better conversion rates/_____)?

3. In what ways have our sales stories developed to better reflect the (current market demands/client expectations/_____) based on collective feedback?

4. How often should we review and update our sales narratives to ensure they remain (relevant/compelling/_____) to our target audience?

5. What challenges have you encountered when trying to refine sales narratives, and how did you (overcome them/adapt/_____)?

(5) Salesperson to External Stakeholders or Partners:

1. What (strategies/methodologies/_____) have you found most effective in measuring the success of shared sales stories?

2. Can we exchange insights on how to enhance our (storytelling approaches/engagement techniques/_____) based on mutual feedback?

3. How do shifts in (consumer preferences/industry dynamics/_____) influence your evaluation of sales narrative effectiveness?

4. What are the prospects for conducting joint (seminars/feedback sessions/_____) to refine our storytelling based on collective insights?

5. How can we integrate our unique selling propositions into unified stories that captivate our shared market segments?

B.   TRACKING ENGAGEMENT AND CONVERSION METRICS:

These questions aim to gauge and enhance the effectiveness of sales narratives. Perfect for post-campaign analyses or strategic planning sessions. They help you assess how your storytelling influences customer engagement and conversions. Use these questions to gather insights for refining sales techniques, ensuring narratives resonate more deeply with audiences, and drive better sales outcomes.

(1) Salesperson to Client:

1. How do you track the impact of our sales narratives on your (engagement/conversion rates/_____) with our solutions?

2. Can you share any (metrics/insights/_____) on how our storytelling has influenced your decision-making process?

3. Have you noticed any specific (content/themes/_____) in our sales narratives that particularly resonated with your team?

4. What methods do you use to measure the effectiveness of the sales narratives we provide in terms of (lead generation/customer retention/_____)?

5. Could you provide feedback on which part of our sales presentation (captivated/lost/_____) your interest and why?

6. How have our sales stories impacted your (understanding/perception/_____) of our product's value?

7. In terms of conversion, which aspects of our narrative do you think could be (enhanced/modified/_____) to better meet your needs?

8. Are there any (tools/technologies/_____) you've found effective in tracking the (engagement/conversion/_____) impact of sales narratives on your end?

9. Have you implemented any (changes/actions/_____) based on our sales stories, and how have these impacted your (operations/sales figures/_____)?

10. Would you be willing to participate in a (survey/interview/_____) to provide more detailed feedback on our sales narratives' effectiveness?

(2) Client to Salesperson:

1. What (metrics/indicators/_____) do you use to determine the success of your sales narratives in engaging clients like us?

2. How do you collect and analyze (customer feedback/sales data/_____) to refine your sales stories for better (engagement/conversion/_____)?

3. Can you show examples of how changes in your sales narrative have led to improved (customer engagement/conversion rates/_____)?

4. What strategies do you recommend for us to track the impact of sales narratives on our (purchase decisions/customer journey/_____)?

5. How frequently do you (update/revise/_____) your sales narratives based on engagement and conversion metrics?

6. In what ways can we collaborate to measure the effectiveness of your sales stories in achieving our (specific goals/target outcomes/_____)?

7. Are there any (tools/platforms/_____) you suggest we use to better understand how your sales narratives influence our engagement with your product?

8. How can you assist us in setting up a system to track the (ROI/impact/_____) of the sales narratives on our decision-making process?

9. What (benchmarks/best practices/_____) do you follow to ensure your sales narratives are continuously (improving/resonating/_____) with clients?

10. How do you integrate (client feedback/market trends/_____) into developing your sales narratives for maximum impact on engagement and conversions?

(3) Salesperson to Self:

1. What specific (metrics/indicators/_____) am I tracking to measure the impact of my sales stories on (engagement/conversions/_____)?

2. How frequently should I review and update my sales narratives to ensure they remain (relevant/effective/_____)?

3. In what areas can I improve my storytelling techniques to drive higher (engagement rates/conversion rates/_____)?

4. How can I more effectively measure the ROI of my sales narratives to ensure they are contributing to (sales goals/client satisfaction/_____)?

5. What (tools/resources/_____) can I leverage to gain deeper insights into how my sales narratives impact (customer decisions/customer satisfaction/_____)?

(4) Salesperson to Colleagues/Internal Team:

1. What (tools/methodologies/_____) are we using to track the engagement and conversion metrics related to our sales stories?

2. What best practices have we identified for integrating (real-time feedback/analytics/_____) into our storytelling approach?

3. How can we better collaborate to ensure our sales narratives are continuously updated to reflect (market changes/customer insights/_____)?

4. In our team discussions, how are we leveraging insights from (social media engagement/sales performance metrics/_____) to refine our narratives?

5. What challenges have we faced in measuring the impact of our sales stories, and how can we overcome them?

(5) Salesperson to External Stakeholders or Partners:

1. How can our partnership leverage (analytics tools/data sharing/_____) to better track the engagement and conversion metrics of our combined sales narratives?

2. What insights have you gained from your experience with measuring the impact of sales stories that could help us enhance our approach?

3. How can we collaborate on creating a unified approach to (collecting/analyzing/_____) engagement and conversion data from our sales narratives?

4. How can our sales narratives be adjusted based on the (conversion metrics/engagement data/_____) we collect through our partnership?

5. What opportunities do you see for improving the tracking of (engagement/conversion metrics/_____) to make our storytelling more impactful?

14. LEVERAGING TECHNOLOGY AND CRM SYSTEMS

A.   INTEGRATION OF SALES TECHNOLOGIES:

Navigating the complexities of modern sales demands a mastery of technology and CRM systems. This collection of questions is crafted to explore the customization, integration, and adoption of these tools, ensuring they meet unique business needs and enhance customer interactions. Suitable for you looking to refine your tech use, these inquiries help pinpoint areas for improvement, driving efficiency and fostering stronger customer relationships in a digital-first sales environment.

(1) Salesperson to Client:

1. How can our (CRM system/sales automation tools/_____) be tailored to better meet your (service expectations/communication preferences/_____)?

2. What specific (features/functionality/_____) of our CRM would you find most beneficial for managing your (customer interactions/sales processes/_____)?

3. Can you share how integration of our CRM with your (marketing automation/customer service platforms/_____) could streamline your workflows?

4. How important is (training/adoption/_____) support to you when implementing new sales technologies?

5. In what ways can we customize the (data reports/analytics dashboards/_____) in our CRM to provide you with insights on (customer behavior/sales trends/_____)?

6. Would you be interested in exploring how our CRM's (mobile access/cloud capabilities/_____) can enhance your team's (productivity/mobility/_____)?

7. How can the (customization/configuration/_____) options of our CRM improve your (data management/lead tracking/_____) processes?

8. What challenges do you expect in integrating our CRM with your existing (business systems/workflows/_____), and how can we assist?

9. How do you see our (sales automation software/data analytics platforms/_____) affecting your (customer engagement/sales strategy/_____) in the long term?

10. What (training modules/educational resources/_____) can we provide to ensure your team fully leverages our CRM's (automation features/integration capabilities/_____)?

(2) Client to Salesperson:

1. Can you explain how the (CRM system/sales automation software/_____) can be customized to fit our specific (industry needs/business model/_____)?

2. What are the key benefits of integrating your CRM with our (marketing automation/customer service platforms/_____)?

3. How does your team support (training/adoption/_____) for new users of your sales technologies?

4. Are there any (integration challenges/compatibility issues/_____) we should know when using your CRM alongside our existing systems?

5. What kind of (data analytics/reporting capabilities/_____) does your CRM offer to help us understand our (customer base/sales performance/_____) better?

6. How can your CRM enhance our team's (productivity/efficiency/_____) through its (mobile access/cloud features/_____)?

7. What kind of (customization options/configuration tools/_____) are available within your CRM to adapt to our (workflow preferences/data management needs/_____)?

8. How do you ensure the (security/privacy/_____) of our data within your CRM and sales technologies?

9. Can you provide (case studies/examples/_____) of how businesses like ours have successfully leveraged your CRM for (customer engagement/sales growth/_____)?

10. What are the (support options/training resources/_____) available to us post-implementation of your sales technologies?

(3) Salesperson to Self:

1. Have I fully understood the (customization/configuration/_____) capabilities of our CRM to meet diverse client needs?

2. How can I improve my knowledge on integrating our CRM with other (business systems/platforms/_____) to provide better solutions to clients?

3. What steps can I take to ensure I'm proficient in explaining the benefits of our (sales automation tools/data analytics platforms/_____) to clients?

4. Am I effectively communicating the value of (training/adoption support/_____) when introducing our CRM and sales technologies?

5. How can I stay updated on the latest (CRM features/technology trends/_____) to remain a valuable resource for my clients?

(4) Salesperson to Colleagues/Internal Team:

1. How can we collaborate to enhance our knowledge of (CRM customization/technology integration/_____) for better client support?

2. What best practices have we identified for encouraging high (adoption rates/training engagement/_____) among our CRM users?

3. Can we share insights on overcoming common challenges with CRM (integration/implementation/_____) faced by our clients?

4. How do we ensure we're providing comprehensive (support/training/_____) for the technologies we offer?

5. What strategies can we employ to keep our team updated on the latest advancements in (CRM capabilities/sales automation/_____)?

(5) Salesperson to External Stakeholders or Partners:

1. How can we collaborate to enhance the (integration capabilities/customization options/_____) of our CRM for mutual clients?

2. What insights can you share from your experience with (CRM systems/sales technologies/_____) that could benefit our product development?

3. Are there opportunities for us to integrate our CRM with your (platforms/services/_____) to offer a more comprehensive solution to clients?

4. How can we leverage your (expertise/technologies/_____) to improve our CRM's (data analytics/reporting/_____) features?

5. What (training resources/support mechanisms/_____) do you offer that can assist in the adoption and effective use of our combined solutions?

b. DIGITAL AND SOCIAL SELLING:

Navigating the digital sales landscape requires effective use of CRM systems and sales technologies. These questions are aimed at understanding how to best integrate, customize, and use these tools to streamline sales processes and enhance engagement. They're designed for you looking to maximize the benefits of technology in sales, ensuring systems meet specific team needs, improve workflows, and foster a unified customer view, all while ensuring high adoption rates through comprehensive training.

1) Salesperson to Client:

1. How can our (social media platforms/email marketing campaigns/_____) better serve your interests and keep you informed about (industry trends/new products/_____)?

2. In what ways can we enhance our online content to provide you with valuable insights on (market developments/product usage/_____)?

3. Would you find value in personalized (brand stories/product demonstrations/_____) shared through our digital channels?

4. How can we leverage our digital presence to support your decision-making process in (product selection/strategic planning/_____)?

5. Are there specific (digital formats/channels/_____) you prefer to receive updates and engaging with our brand?

6. How important is it for you to see our sales professionals actively sharing their expertise and insights on (LinkedIn/Twitter/_____)?

7. What type of (content/themes/_____) do you find most engaging and helpful on our social media platforms?

8. Can we provide you with (exclusive access/early previews/_____) through our digital and social selling channels?

9. How can our digital and social selling efforts make it easier for you to (share feedback/connect with peers/_____) related to our products?

10. Would you appreciate (live Q&A sessions/webinars/_____) featuring our product experts and industry thought leaders?

(2) Client to Salesperson:

1. Can you recommend how I can stay updated with your latest (product releases/industry insights/_____) through social media?

2. What (digital tools/social platforms/_____) do you use to ensure clients receive personalized and relevant content?

3. How do you ensure the credibility and accuracy of the information shared on your (social media channels/email newsletters/_____)?

4. Are there opportunities for me to engage with your brand or provide feedback through your digital channels?

5. What measures do you take to protect client privacy and data security on your digital and social selling platforms?

6. Can you provide examples of how your digital content strategy has helped clients in making informed (purchase decisions/strategic changes/_____)?

7. How do your social listening tools enhance your understanding of (client needs/market trends/_____)?

8. What kind of support do you offer through your digital channels for (post-purchase inquiries/product training/_____)?

9. How does your brand's digital presence facilitate building (personal connections/professional connections/_____) and trust between sales professionals and clients?

10. Are there (referral incentives/loyalty programs/_____) that I can take advantage of through your digital platforms?

(3) Salesperson to Self:

1. Have I effectively used (social media/email marketing/_____) to nurture leads and engage with my prospects?

2. How can I improve my personal brand on social media to position myself as a (thought leader/industry expert/_____)?

3. Am I adequately leveraging social listening to stay informed about (brand mentions/competitor activities/_____)?

4. What new (content strategies/digital tools/_____) can I adopt to enhance my engagement with clients and prospects?

5. How can I better integrate my sales strategies with digital and social selling to achieve (higher conversions/more personalized engagement/_____)?

(4) Salesperson to Colleagues/Internal Team:

1. How can we collaborate to ensure that we align our (social media content/email campaigns/_____) and consistently provide value to our audience?

2. What successes have we seen from integrating personal branding efforts of our sales team into our overall digital selling strategy?

3. Can we share insights on effective (social listening/social media/_____) practices that have helped us better understand our (clients'/market's/_____) needs?

4. How can we further tailor our (content strategy/social media strategy/_____) to address the specific interests and challenges of our target audience?

5. What (training/resources/_____) are needed to enhance our team's proficiency in digital and social selling techniques?

(5) Salesperson to External Stakeholders or Partners:

1. How can our partnership amplify our digital and social selling efforts, particularly in providing (joint content/cross-promotional opportunities/_____)?

2. What (tools/platforms/_____) do you recommend for enhancing our social listening and engagement strategies?

3. Can you share examples of successful digital or social selling campaigns that we could model or adapt?

4. How can we use your experience to improve our content strategy for (lead nurturing/customer education/_____)?

5. Are there opportunities for co-creating (content/digital experiences/_____) that could benefit both our brands and our shared audience?

c. **ADDITIONAL CONSIDERATIONS:**

Navigating the evolving landscape of sales technology requires a keen understanding of how tools like CRM systems, AI, and mobile applications can enhance customer relationships and sales efficiency. These questions aim to guide you in assessing and maximizing the impact of these technologies on your sales strategies. They address integration, customization, adoption, and data security, providing a roadmap for leveraging technology to improve sales outcomes and build stronger customer connections.

(1) Salesperson to Client:

1. How could our (mobile sales tools/AI-driven recommendations/_____) improve your access to (product information/real-time updates/_____) while on the go?

2. In what ways can we enhance your experience with our (CRM system/analytics platform/_____) to support your (decision-making processes/customer engagement/_____)?

3. Are there specific (data privacy/security measures/_____) you're concerned about when using our (sales technologies/CRM systems/_____)?

4. How important is (predictive analytics/lead scoring/_____) powered by AI in refining your (sales/operations/_____) strategy?

5. Can we provide you with more detailed (analytics/reporting tools/_____) to better understand your sales performance and customer behaviors?

6. Would you be interested in training sessions on how to maximize the use of (AI tools/mobile applications/_____) for (sales/operational/_____) efficiency?

7. How can integrating our CRM system with your (marketing automation/customer service platforms/_____) streamline your business processes?

8. What improvements would you suggest for our (data analytics/reports/_____) to make them more actionable for your team?

9. How can we make our (mobile sales applications/CRM system/_____) more user-friendly for your daily sales activities?

10. Are there additional features you'd like to see in our (CRM system/mobile sales tools/_____) that could further benefit your sales team?

(2) Client to Salesperson:

1. What mobile (sales/operations/_____) tools do you offer that can help me manage my (sales/operations/_____) tasks more efficiently?

2. Can you explain how your CRM system uses (AI/chatbots/_____) to provide personalized customer interactions?

3. What data (privacy/security/_____) protocols are in place to protect my customer information within your CRM?

4. How does your CRM provide (analytics/reporting/_____) to help forecast sales and understand customer behaviors?

5. Are there options for customizing your CRM system to fit my specific (sales/business development/_____) workflow and data needs?

6. What kind of (training/support/_____) do you offer for adopting new sales technologies and CRM systems?

7. How do your sales technologies integrate with other business systems for a more cohesive view of customer interactions?

8. Can you show me how to use (mobile sales/email marketing/_____) applications to access information and perform tasks remotely?

9. What advancements in (AI/machine learning/_____) within your sales tools should I be aware of for future planning?

10. How do you ensure ongoing (updates/improvements/_____) to your CRM system to meet growing sales needs?

(3) Salesperson to Self:

1. Have I fully leveraged our CRM's (analytics tools/predictive capabilities/_____) to enhance my sales strategy?

2. Am I up-to-date on the latest (mobile sales applications/AI technologies/_____) that could improve my sales performance?

3. How can I better ensure data (privacy/security/_____) when using our sales technologies with customer information?

4. What additional (training/resources/_____) do I need to use more effectively our (CRM/sales/_____) technologies?

5. How can I facilitate better integration of our CRM with other business systems to streamline my (sales/cold calling/_____) process?

(4) Salesperson to Colleagues/Internal Team:

1. How can we collaborate to customize our CRM system to better meet our team's specific (needs/workflows/_____)?

2. What successes have we seen from using (mobile sales tools/AI features/_____) in our sales processes?

3. Can we share best practices for ensuring data (privacy/security/_____) when using our (sales/CRM/_____) technologies?

4. How have analytics and reporting from our CRM system impacted our sales (strategies/outcomes/_____)?

5. What (training/support/_____) do we need to improve our adoption and utilization of new sales technologies?

(5) Salesperson to External Stakeholders or Partners:

1. How can we collaborate to integrate our CRM system with your platforms for a more unified customer engagement strategy?

2. Can you share insights on leveraging (AI/machine learning/_____) in (sales/product development/_____) technologies for predictive analytics and personalization?

3. What are the action plans for ensuring data privacy and security within (CRM systems/sales technologies/_____)?

4. How can we use (analytics/reporting/_____) features within our CRM to better understand and serve our mutual customers?

5. Are there opportunities for co-developing (mobile sales tools/AI-driven sales applications/_____) that could benefit both our organizations?

15. ETHICAL SELLING AND TRANSPARENCY

A.   ETHICAL CONSIDERATIONS:

These questions guide you in fostering ethical practices and transparency throughout the sales process. They're crafted to encourage thoughtful consideration of honesty, integrity, customer autonomy, and fair competition in dealings with clients and competitors alike. Use them to assess and improve upon how ethical considerations are integrated into sales strategies, ensuring a commitment to upholding customer trust, data privacy, and the ethical standards that define responsible business conduct.

(1) Salesperson to Client:

1. How can we improve our communication to ensure you feel fully (informed/confident/_____) in your decisions regarding our (products/services/_____)?

2. In what ways can we better show our commitment to (protecting your data/respecting your confidentiality/_____)?

3. Are there (practices/standards/_____) you expect from us to ensure fair competition and the integrity of our offerings compared to others in the market?

4. How can we make our sales processes more transparent to help you understand the (value/ethics/_____) behind our (products/services/_____)?

5. Do you have suggestions for how we can further respect customer autonomy, ensuring you never feel (undue pressure/overwhelmed/_____) from our sales team?

6. How can we provide you with clearer (insights/reasoning/_____) into our pricing structure and product development process to enhance (transparency/trust/_____)?

7. Are there specific areas where you feel more (information/clarity/_____) would enable you to make better-informed decisions about our offerings?

8. How do you prefer to be informed about how we use and protect your data, and are there improvements we can make to our current communication process?

9. In your view, what actions can we take to show our unwavering commitment to (ethical/trustworthy/_____) practices in our (sales/marketing/_____) efforts?

10. Would detailed (case studies/testimonials/_____) from other clients about their experiences with our (ethical practices/transparency/_____) be helpful in building your confidence in our partnership?

(2) Client to Salesperson:

1. Can you explain the measures your company takes to ensure (honesty/integrity/_____) in all customer dealings?

2. How does your organization ensure compliance with data protection (laws/best practices/_____) and maintain customer confidentiality?

3. What policies do you have in place to guarantee (fair competition/ethical treatment/_____) of competitors?

4. How do you ensure that your sales team is (trained/knowledgeable/_____) about ethical selling practices?

5. Can you provide examples of how your commitment to ethical selling has guided your approach to (resolving customer issues/business development/_____)?

6. How does your company handle situations where product capabilities might not fully meet a client's expectations?

7. In what ways do you ensure transparency about product (pricing fees/additional costs/_____)?

8. What steps does your organization take to avoid conflicts of interest in sales transactions?

9. How are ethical considerations integrated into your (sales goals/performance evaluations/_____)?

10. Can you describe a situation where your company prioritized (ethical/fairness/_____) considerations over potential revenue?

(3) Salesperson to Self:

1. Have I consistently upheld the highest ethical standards in my interactions with clients, even when faced with challenging (sales targets/customers/_____)?

2. What steps can I take to enhance my (understanding/application/_____) of (data privacy/security/_____) measures in my sales activities?

3. How can I better advocate for (customer autonomy/informed decision-making/_____) in my sales approach?

4. In what ways can I contribute to fostering a culture of ethical selling within my (team/organization/_____)?

5. How can I ensure that I remain up-to-date with (laws/regulations/_____) governing ethical selling practices in my industry?

(4) Salesperson to Colleagues/Internal Team:

1. How can we collectively ensure that our sales practices reflect the highest (ethical standards/transparency/_____) with clients?

2. What strategies can we implement to (better protect customer data/uphold confidentiality/_____) across all our sales activities?

3. How can we support each other in maintaining ethical standards and avoiding (undue pressure/manipulative tactics/_____) in our sales approach?

4. What measures can we take as a team to (monitor/improve/_____) our adherence to fair competition principles continuously?

5. Can we share examples of (ethical dilemmas/ethical complaints/_____) we've faced in our sales roles and discuss how we navigated them while maintaining integrity?

(5) Salesperson to External Stakeholders or Partners:

1. How can our partnership reinforce ethical selling practices and ensure transparency in our combined offerings with customers?

2. Are there collaborative (initiatives/workshops/_____) we can undertake to enhance data (privacy/security/_____) measures for our customers?

3. How do you approach ethical considerations in your (marketing/sales/_____) practices, and what lessons can we learn from each other?

4. In what ways can we work together to set industry standards for (ethical selling/fair competition/_____)?

5. Can we share (resources/training programs/_____) that have been effective in promoting ethical selling practices within our organizations?

B.   BUILDING TRUST THROUGH TRANSPARENCY:

These questions are crafted to guide sales professionals in reinforcing ethical selling practices and nurturing trust through transparency. They serve as a tool for conversations with clients, team members, and partners about honesty, integrity, and the clear communication of product details and limitations. Use these inquiries across different interactions to commit to ethical standards, respect customer decisions, and ensure accurate and consistent information delivery.

(1) Salesperson to Client:

1. How can we better communicate our (product's capabilities/limitations/_____) to ensure your expectations are accurately set from the start?

2. Would (detailed case studies/examples/_____) where our product might not be the best fit help you in making more informed decisions?

3. How can we improve our (pricing transparency/value understanding/_____) to make sure you fully understand the value of our offerings?

4. In what ways can we enhance our (after-sale support communication/warranties and guarantees information/_____) to ensure you are fully aware of (warranties/guarantees/_____)?

5. Is there (additional information/specific details/_____) you need about our (product/service/_____) that would make you feel more confident in your purchasing decision?

6. In what ways can we provide more (clarity/comparative insights/_____) about how our (products/services/_____) compare to others in the market, ensuring you feel informed without disparaging our competitors?

7. How can we improve our communication about the (ongoing support/updates/_____) you can expect after your purchase, to ensure there are no surprises?

8. Would it be valuable for us to provide a (transparent breakdown/insightful overview/_____) of our product's development process, highlighting how we integrate customer feedback into improvements?

9. How can we better inform you about the (ethical sourcing/social responsibility initiatives/_____) related to our (products/services/_____)?

10. What format of communication do you prefer for receiving (updates/changes in terms/_____), conditions, or policies that could affect your use of our (product/service/_____)?

(2) Client to Salesperson:

1. Can you provide an (honest assessment/clear overview/_____) of how your (product/service/_____) aligns with our specific needs, including any potential limitations?

2. How do you ensure all (information/details/_____) provided before the sale is (consistent/accurate/_____) and continues to be so after the purchase?

3. What are the most common (questions/concerns/_____) customers have after purchasing, and how are these addressed?

4. How (transparent/open/_____) is your company about (product development/updates/_____), especially regarding features that may affect us?

5. Can you explain your company's approach to (data protection/information security/_____) and how my information will be safeguarded?

6. What steps does your company take to (maintain/build/_____) trust with customers throughout the sales process and beyond?

7. How are (customer feedback/suggestions/_____) incorporated into your (product development/service improvements/_____)?

8. Can you detail the measures in place for ensuring (customer autonomy/privacy/_____) in your sales and marketing practices?

9. What policies do you have for (addressing/resolving/_____) discrepancies between promised and delivered (features/services/_____)?

10. How does your company communicate (changes/updates/_____) to terms, conditions, or policies that could affect how I use your (product/service/_____)?

(3) Salesperson to Self:

1. Am I fully transparent with clients about the (strengths/potential limitations/_____) of our (products/services/_____)?

2. How can I better prepare to discuss our product's (pricing/value proposition/_____) clearly and honestly?

3. In what areas do I need more (knowledge/training/_____) to provide accurate and consistent information to clients?

4. How can I ensure that I'm fully respecting the client's (autonomy/right/_____) to make an informed decision?

5. What steps can I take to continuously improve my approach to (ethical selling/transparency/_____) in all client interactions?

(4) Salesperson to Colleagues/Internal Team:

1. How can we collaborate to maintain consistency in our messaging across all (platforms/customer touchpoints/_____)?

2. What best practices can we share for discussing our product's limitations honestly while still highlighting its value?

3. How can we better support each other in delivering exceptional (after-sale/customer support /_____) service that aligns with our initial promises?

4. What strategies have you found effective in building (long-term relationships/trust/_____) with clients through transparency?

5. Can we establish a regular review of our (sales materials/sales processes/_____) to ensure they meet the highest ethical standards?

(5) Salesperson to External Stakeholders or Partners:

1. How can our partnership further enhance (transparency/ethical/_____) selling practices with our mutual clients?

2. Are there (tools/technologies/_____) you recommend that can help us improve transparency in our sales process?

3. How do you approach full disclosure and honesty in your sales practices, and what (do/don't/_____) lessons can we learn from each other?

4. What measures do you take to protect customer data, and how can we align our (work/practices/_____) to ensure a unified standard?

5. Can we collaborate on creating content that (educates/inspires/_____) customers on the importance of (transparency/ethical/_____) considerations in sales?

C.   ADDITIONAL CONSIDERATIONS:

These questions are crafted to guide discussions on ethical selling and transparency within the sales process. Aimed at reinforcing integrity, customer respect, and accountability, they encourage exploration of how sales practices can embody ethical principles, ensure data protection, and promote fairness. Ideal for dialogue with clients, self-reflection, team collaboration, and partnership building, these inquiries help solidify a commitment to ethical standards, fostering trust and loyalty among all stakeholders.

(1) Salesperson to Client:

1. How can we better communicate our commitment to (ethical training/an ethical culture/_____) within our organization to you, our valued client?

2. In what ways can we show our ongoing efforts towards (sustainability/social responsibility/_____) in our (sales/marketing/_____) practices that matter most to you?

3. Would more transparent reporting on our (monitoring/enforcement/_____) of ethical sales practices increase your trust in our brand?

4. How important is it for you that our sales approach considers not just your needs but also the broader impact on (community stakeholders/the environment/_____)?

5. Can we provide (examples/case studies/_____) showing how our ethical considerations in sales have led to positive outcomes for (clients/communities/_____)?

6. How can we better illustrate our commitment to ethical practices in every interaction you have with our (sales/customer support/_____) team, ensuring you feel fully informed and respected throughout the (sales/client relationship/_____) process?

7. Would you appreciate updates on our continuous efforts towards (ethical training/ethical company culture/_____) and the fostering of an integrity-based sales culture, and how frequently would you like to receive such information?

8. How can we make our (sustainability efforts/social responsibility/_____) initiatives more visible to you, and in what ways could this influence your decision-making regarding our (products/services/_____)?

9. What additional steps could we take to ensure that our commitment to (ethical selling/transparency/_____) is clear and unequivocal in all our (communications/marketing materials/_____)?

10. Are there specific areas within our sales practices where you feel a stronger emphasis on (ethical considerations/sustainability measures/_____) could be beneficial, both for you as a client and for the (wider community/environment/_____)?

(2) Client to Salesperson:

1. How does your company's (ethical training/cultural values/_____) guide interactions and decision-making in sales engagements with clients like us?

2. What (mechanisms/policies/_____) does your organization employ to (monitor/enforce/_____) ethical sales practices, including handling reports of unethical behavior?

3. In what ways do you engage (stakeholders/partners/_____) to ensure ethical considerations extend beyond your sales team to all aspects of your operations?

4. How do you integrate (sustainability/social responsibility/_____) into your sales strategies, reflecting a commitment to ethical practices?

5. Can you explain how your team uses client feedback to improve (ethical standards/sales methodologies/_____)?

6. How does your organization ensure transparency and honesty in all client communications, particularly regarding (product limitations/service commitments/_____)?

7. What role does (stakeholder feedback/employee involvement/_____) play in shaping the ethical culture and sales practices of your company?

8. How are new sales representatives trained on the importance of (data privacy/customer respect/_____) as part of their onboarding process?

9. Can you provide examples of how your company has adapted its sales approach to better align with (ethical guidelines/sustainability goals/_____)?

10. How does your company balance competitive sales tactics with maintaining a high standard of (ethical conduct/client trust/_____)?

(3) Salesperson to Self:

1. How regularly do I engage with (ethical training materials/professional development resources/_____), and how does this knowledge influence my (sales approach/customer interactions/_____)?

2. What steps can I take to ensure that my (sales practices/client engagements/_____) are not only effective but also (ethically sound/transparent/_____)?

3. How do I balance the pursuit of (sales targets/competitive achievements/_____) with the need to respect (customer autonomy/ethical considerations/_____)?

4. In what ways can I contribute to a culture of (ethical selling/team collaboration/_____) within my (team/broader organization/_____)?

5. How can I better incorporate principles of (sustainability/social responsibility/_____) into my daily (sales interactions/client communications/_____)?

(4) Salesperson to Colleagues/Internal Team:

1. How can we collaboratively strengthen our (ethical training/culture of integrity/_____) and foster a culture that prioritizes (integrity/ethical behavior/_____) in sales?

2. What best practices can we establish for (monitoring our sales activities/ensuring alignment with ethical guidelines/_____) and ensuring they align with our (ethical guidelines/core values/_____)?

3. How can we better engage with all (stakeholders/partners/_____) to ensure our (sales practices/business operations/_____) have a positive impact?

4. In what ways can we collectively contribute to the company's (sustainability/social responsibility/_____) goals through our (sales strategies/marketing efforts/_____)?

5. How can we support each other in maintaining consistency in our (ethical messaging/commitments to clients/_____) and (commitments to clients/promises of integrity/_____)?

(5) Salesperson to External Stakeholders or Partners:

1. How can we work together to enhance (ethical training/culture/_____) across our partnership to benefit our (mutual clients/shared audiences/_____)?

2. What joint initiatives could we undertake to (monitor/enforce/_____) ethical practices within our (sales and marketing efforts/collaborative projects/_____)?

3. How can our collaboration extend (ethical considerations/positive impacts/_____) to all stakeholders, ensuring (positive impacts/beneficial outcomes/_____) on (employees/partners/_____), and (communities/ecosystems/_____)?

4. In what ways can we integrate (sustainability/social responsibility/_____) more deeply into our combined (sales practices/business strategies/_____)?

5. Can we share (tools/resources/_____), or (methodologies/approaches/_____) that have been effective in promoting (ethical selling/transparency/_____) within our respective organizations?

16. CONSULTATIVE SELLING AND PROBLEM SOLVING

A. SHIFTING FROM SELLING TO CONSULTING:

Transitioning to a consultative selling approach enhances client relationships by focusing on solving their unique challenges. These questions guide you through various interactions, from understanding client needs to refining personal and team strategies. Whether dealing with clients, self-evaluation, internal teamwork, or external partnerships, this set prepares you to shift from transactional selling to becoming a trusted advisor, ensuring your engagements are deeply rooted in empathy, active listening, and tailored solutions.

(1) For Salesperson to Client:

1. How can we improve the alignment of our (solutions/offerings/_____) to directly address your current (challenges/goals/_____)?

2. In what ways can I enhance my (listening/empathy/_____) to fully understand your (needs/expectations/_____)?

3. What specific (obstacles/concerns/_____) are you facing that we can explore (solutions/options/_____) for?

4. How do you envision a (partnership/relationship/_____) with our company supporting your long-term (objectives/growth/_____)?

5. Can you share examples where a (product/service/_____) fell short of meeting your needs, and how you wish it was handled?

6. What are the key (values/principles/_____) that you look for in a (supplier/partner/_____), and how can we embody those?

7. How would you describe the ideal (outcome/solution/_____) for your current (challenge/project/_____)?

8. Can we delve deeper into how your (industry/market/_____) is changing and the implications for your (strategy/operations/_____)?

9. What has been your experience with (consultative selling/previous suppliers/_____), and how can we improve upon it?

10. In what areas are you seeking more than just a (vendor/supplier/_____), but a (consultant/advisor/_____) who can add strategic value?

(2) For Client to Salesperson:

1. Can you show how your (products/services/_____) have solved problems for others in my (industry/sector/_____)?

2. What specific (training/support/_____) do you provide to ensure we fully leverage your (solutions/technology/_____)?

3. How does your company stay informed about (market trends/customer needs/_____) to continually adapt your (offerings/strategies/_____)?

4. Could you walk me through a case where your consultative approach directly contributed to a client's (success/growth/_____)?

5. How do you ensure that your (advice/recommendations/_____) are always (aligned with/objective towards/_____) our best interests?

6. How can your (team/technology/_____) adapt to our evolving (business needs/market demands/_____) over time?

7. Can you explain how your approach to (consultative selling/problem-solving/_____) sets you apart from competitors in our (industry/niche/_____)?

8. What success metrics do you use to evaluate the effectiveness of your (solutions/strategies/_____) in addressing specific client (challenges/outcomes/_____)?

9. How do you ensure that your sales team remains (knowledgeable/up-to-date/_____) on (industry trends/product advancements/_____) to provide relevant advice?

10. What steps do you take to maintain (transparency/accountability/_____) throughout the sales process, especially when (challenges/changes/_____) arise?

(3) For Salesperson to Self:

1. Am I dedicating enough time to (research/understand/_____) my clients' industries and specific (challenges/opportunities/_____)?

2. How can I improve my (active listening/empathy/_____) to better understand and respond to client (needs/concerns/_____)?

3. In what ways can I expand my (knowledge/skills/_____) to offer more insightful (advice/solutions/_____) to clients?

4. Am I effectively building (trust/relationships/_____) with clients by focusing on long-term (success/value/_____) rather than immediate sales?

5. How can I better use (diagnostic questions/feedback/_____) to tailor my approach to each client's unique (situation/requirements/_____)?

(4) For Salesperson to Colleagues/Internal Team:

1. How can we collaborate more effectively to ensure our (solutions/strategies/_____) are fully (customized/aligned/_____) with client needs?

2. What resources or (training/techniques/_____) have you found valuable for improving your consultative selling (skills/approach/_____)?

3. Can we share insights on (success stories/challenges/_____) to enhance our collective ability to solve client (problems/needs/_____)?

4. How do we ensure our team remains (up-to-date/educated/_____) on industry trends to better serve our clients' (evolving/dynamic/_____) needs?

5. What mechanisms do we have in place for (gathering/leveraging/_____) customer (feedback/insights/_____) to improve our consultative approach?

(5) For Salesperson to External Stakeholders or Partners:

1. In what ways can we (collaborate/partner/_____) to bring additional value to our clients through (joint solutions/innovations/_____)?

2. How have you incorporated (active listening/empathy/_____) into your sales process, and what impact has it had on your client relationships?

3. Can you share examples of how diagnostic questions have helped you (uncover/solve/_____) deeper client (challenges/needs/_____)?

4. How can we leverage each other's (strengths/expertise/_____) to foster stronger, long-term relationships with our clients?

5. What (strategies/tools/_____) have you found effective in ensuring a consistent, ethical approach to (selling/engaging with/_____) clients?

b. VALUE-BASED SELLING:

Value-based selling shifts the focus from the product to the customer's unique needs and desired outcomes. This set of questions is crafted to assist you in deeply understanding your clients' challenges, presenting tailored value propositions, and nurturing long-term relationships. It covers interactions with clients, self-assessment, team collaboration, and partner engagements, all aiming to prioritize the delivery of significant, strategic value over mere transactional exchanges.

(1) Salesperson to Client:

1. How can our (solutions/strategies/_____) address your unique (challenges/goals/_____) more effectively than other options you've considered?

2. In what ways can we tailor our (services/products/_____) to better align with your (industry/needs/_____)?

3. Can you share how you measure (success/outcomes/_____) so we can show the specific value our (solutions/technologies/_____) offer?

4. How do you foresee our (product/service/_____) changing with your business to meet future (challenges/goals/_____)?

5. What outcomes are most critical to your (strategy/business/_____), and how can we align our (solutions/value proposition/_____) accordingly?

6. Could you detail a scenario where understanding more about (emerging trends/potential needs/_____) might change your approach to (purchasing/strategy/_____)?

7. How do our (solutions/services/_____) align with your long-term (vision/goals/_____)?

8. In what areas do you see our (product/service/_____) adding the most value to your (operations/business model/_____)?

9. Can we explore potential (barriers/limitations/_____) you foresee with our (solution/product/_____), and how we might address them?

10. What specific (features/elements/_____) of our (product/service/_____) do you find most valuable for your (business/strategy/_____)?

(2) Client to Salesperson:

1. How does your (product/service/_____) differ from competitors in terms of (value/impact/_____) for a business like ours?

2. Can you provide examples of how your (solutions/technologies/_____) have adapted to changing (industry needs/customer demands/_____)?

3. What ongoing (support/training/_____) do you offer to ensure we continue to see value from your (product/service/_____)?

4. How do you (measure/quantify/_____) the impact of your (solutions/services/_____) on a client's (ROI/business outcomes/_____)?

5. What kind of (customization/personalization/_____) options are available to ensure your (product/service/_____) meets our specific (needs/requirements/_____)?

6. Can you illustrate how integrating your (product/service/_____) with our existing systems might streamline our (operations/workflows/_____) and enhance overall efficiency?

7. What proactive steps does your company take to understand a client's business before proposing a (solution/strategy/_____)?

8. How does your team stay informed about the latest (industry trends/technological advancements/_____) to ensure the solutions offered remain relevant and valuable?

9. Could you share a success story where your consultative approach significantly impacted a client's (business growth/operational efficiency/_____)?

10. How do you tailor your (services/products/_____) to meet the needs of businesses within our (industry/sector/_____)?

(3) Salesperson to Self:

1. Am I effectively communicating the unique (value/benefits/_____) of our (products/services/_____) to meet the client's (needs/goals/_____)?

2. How can I improve my ability to listen actively and empathize with the customer's (challenges/situation/_____) to provide tailored (solutions/advice/_____)?

3. Do I have sufficient knowledge about the client's (industry/market/_____) to offer (insightful/relevant/_____) advice and (solutions/strategies/_____)?

4. What new (techniques/methods/_____) can I learn to better diagnose a client's (problems/needs/_____) and recommend the most effective (solutions/outcomes/_____)?

5. How can I enhance my approach to building long-term (relationships/trust/_____) with clients through (consistent/dedicated/_____) value-based selling?

(4) Salesperson to Colleagues/Internal Team:

1. How can we collaborate to ensure our (solutions/strategies/_____) are closely aligned with our clients' (needs/goals/_____)?

2. What best practices have we identified in articulating the unique value our (products/services/_____) offer to different (industries/markets/_____)?

3. Can we share successful case studies where our (solutions/products/_____) have developed to meet changing client (needs/demands/_____)?

4. How do we ensure that we equip our entire team to (listen/empathize/_____) with clients and offer (tailored/strategic/_____) advice?

5. What tools or resources can we leverage to better educate our clients on (future needs/potential challenges/_____) and how our (solutions/services/_____) address them?

(5) Salesperson to External Stakeholders or Partners:

1. How can our partnership provide additional (value/support/_____) to our clients through (joint solutions/combined expertise/_____)?

2. Can you share (insights/strategies/_____) that have helped your organization effectively transition from selling to (consulting/problem-solving/_____)?

3. In what ways can we leverage your (technologies/expertise/_____) to enhance our (diagnostic capabilities/listening skills/_____)?

4. What initiatives could we collaborate on to better educate our mutual clients about the long-term (benefits/value/_____) of our (solutions/partnership/_____)?

5. How can we guarantee that our partnership always remains focused on delivering (outcome-based/solution-focused/_____) value to our clients?

c.   ADDITIONAL CONSIDERATIONS:

This collection of questions aids you in transitioning to a consultative selling approach, emphasizing collaborative solution development and adaptability to meet client needs. By focusing on engaging clients in the solution process, these questions support the creation of tailored strategies that align with specific challenges and goals. They encourage reflection, teamwork, and external collaboration to ensure ongoing relevance and effectiveness, fostering long-term, value-driven customer relationships.

(1) Salesperson to Client:

1. How can we work together to tailor our (product/service/_____) to perfectly match your (specific needs/business goals/_____)?

2. What insights can you share about your (industry/challenges/_____) that would help us customize a more effective (solution/strategy/_____) for you?

3. Can you describe a scenario where you needed to rapidly adjust your strategy, and how a flexible (product/service/_____) could have supported you?

4. Would a (proof of concept/pilot program/_____) help you better understand the potential impact of our (solution/technology/_____) on your operations?

5. How frequently would you prefer (follow-up meetings/feedback sessions/_____) to discuss ongoing performance and potential adjustments?

6. In what ways can we incorporate your feedback into the continuous improvement of our (product/service/_____)?

7. What specific (features/functions/_____) are you looking for in a (product/service/_____) that could address your current challenges?

8. How do you envision a (partnership/collaboration/_____) with our team in developing tailored solutions for your business?

9. What (obstacles/limitations/_____) have you encountered with previous solutions, and how can we avoid these in our proposal?

10. How can we ensure our solution remains (flexible/adaptable/_____) to meet your business needs over time?

(2) Client to Salesperson:

1. How do you ensure your (products/services/_____) stay aligned with our customer needs and industry trends?

2. Can you provide examples of how your (solutions/technologies/_____) have adapted to changing market demands?

3. What steps does your company take to collect and implement customer (feedback/suggestions/_____) into your solution development?

4. How does your (product/service/_____) ensure data privacy and security in compliance with current regulations?

5. How are your (analytics/reporting tools/_____) used to measure and enhance customer satisfaction and sales performance?

6. What makes your (consultative approach/solution development process/_____) different from your competitors?

7. Can you explain your process for involving clients in the (solution development/feedback loop/_____)?

8. How do you measure the success of your (consultative selling approach/customer engagements/_____)?

9. What (training/support/_____) do you provide to clients to maximize the value of your (products/services/_____)?

10. How can your (products/services/_____) help us achieve our long-term strategic goals?

(3) Salesperson to Self:

1. How effectively am I using (active listening/diagnostic questions/_____) to truly understand my clients' (needs/challenges/_____)?

2. In what areas can I improve my (flexibility/adaptability/_____) when client needs or situations change unexpectedly?

3. How can I better incorporate client (feedback/insights/_____) into developing more targeted and effective solutions?

4. What steps can I take to enhance my skills in building long-term, trust-based relationships with my clients?

5. How can I ensure I'm staying updated on the latest (industry trends/technological advancements/_____) to offer relevant and valuable consultations?

(4) Salesperson to Colleagues/Internal Team:

1. What can we do to enhance our collaboration and ensure that our solutions are truly customized to each client's unique (needs/situation/_____)?

2. What strategies can we implement to improve our flexibility and adaptability in response to client (feedback/requests/_____)?

3. How can we enhance our approach to providing (proof of concept/pilot programs/_____) that clearly demonstrate value to our clients?

4. In what ways can we strengthen our (follow-up/feedback/_____) mechanisms to keep our solutions aligned with client expectations?

5. How can we foster a culture of (collaboration/continuous improvement/_____) within our team to better support consultative selling?

(5) Salesperson to External Stakeholders or Partners:

1. How can we leverage our partnership to offer more comprehensive and adaptable (solutions/services/_____) to meet client needs?

2. What opportunities do you see for us to collaborate on developing (proof of concept/pilot programs/_____) that demonstrate tangible value?

3. In what ways can we work together to ensure a seamless (integration/collaboration/_____) between our systems for mutual client benefit?

4. How can we establish more effective (follow-up/feedback loops/_____) to continually refine our joint offerings based on customer insights?

5. Can you share insights or technologies that could enhance our ability to adapt and tailor our (solutions/strategies/_____) to client needs more effectively?

17. CROSS-FUNCTIONAL COLLABORATION AND TEAM SELLING

A.   INTERNAL COLLABORATION:

In today's interconnected sales environment, success hinges on seamless collaboration across various functions. This set of questions is designed to foster a synergistic approach, ensuring sales, marketing, product development, and customer service are perfectly aligned. By focusing on unified strategies, effective communication, and shared insights, these questions help create a comprehensive customer experience, enhancing value and building enduring partnerships.

(1) Salesperson to Client:

1. How can our (team's approach/communication strategy/_____) better align with your (current needs/future goals/_____)?

2. In what ways can we incorporate your feedback into our (product development/marketing efforts/_____) to serve you better?

3. How do you see our (product/service/_____) evolving to meet the emerging trends in your (industry/company/_____)?

4. Can you share insights on how our (cross-functional collaboration/customer service/_____) has impacted your experience with us?

5. What additional support can our (technical team/customer service/_____) provide to enhance your usage of our (product/service/_____)?

6. How can our (marketing/sales/_____) teams better communicate the unique (value/benefit/_____) our solutions bring to your business?

7. What are your thoughts on our current (product offerings/communication channels/_____) and how they serve your (needs/requirements/_____)?

8. In our ongoing partnership, how can we improve our (strategy sessions/feedback mechanisms/_____) to better support your objectives?

9. How can we better use insights from our (product development/customer service/_____) teams to address your challenges?

10. How do you envision our (collaborative efforts/internal communication/_____) changing to keep pace with your business (growth/problems/_____)?

(2) Client to Salesperson:

1. How does your (sales/marketing/_____) team incorporate customer (feedback/challenges/_____) into your strategy planning sessions?

2. Can you detail how (customer service/sales/_____) interactions influence your product development roadmap?

3. What (communication channels/methods/_____) do you recommend for providing feedback about my experience with your (products/services/_____)?

4. How do you ensure that (client insights/customer feedback/_____) are effectively communicated across all relevant departments in your company?

5. In what ways can I contribute to the (improvement/evolution/_____) of your services through my (feedback/suggestions/_____)?

6. Could you explain the process for a customer like me to get involved in your (product testing/feedback sessions/_____)?

7. How does your team use customer feedback to (tailor/customize/_____) solutions to meet specific client needs?

8. What initiatives does your company have in place to (gather/analyze/_____) customer feedback across (sales/support/_____) channels?

9. Can you provide examples of how customer (suggestions/feedback/_____) have led to changes in your (products/services/_____)?

10. How frequently does your cross-functional team review (customer feedback/market trends/_____) to adjust your sales and marketing strategies?

(3) Salesperson to Self:

1. How can I better leverage insights from the (marketing/product development/_____) teams to enhance my (sales approach/client solutions/_____)?

2. In what ways can I improve my understanding of our (products/services/_____) to offer more (tailored solutions/specific recommendations/_____) to my clients?

3. How can I foster better communication with (marketing/customer service/_____) to ensure a (seamless customer experience/consistent message/_____)?

4. What steps can I take to stay updated on the latest (product developments/market trends/_____) to inform my (sales strategy/client conversations/_____)?

5. How can I contribute to the (feedback loop/communication channel/_____) between clients and our internal teams to drive (continuous improvement/product evolution/_____)?

(4) Salesperson to Colleagues/Internal Team:

1. How can we align our sales strategies with the latest (marketing campaigns/product updates/_____) to ensure a (cohesive customer journey/unified brand message/_____)?

2. What insights from recent customer feedback can we leverage to adjust our (sales approach/product offerings/_____)?

3. Can we schedule a (joint session/strategy meeting/_____) to discuss how (market trends/customer preferences/_____) are impacting our (sales/marketing/_____) strategies?

4. How can our sales team better support the goals of the (marketing/product development/_____) departments?

5. What are the key takeaways from the latest (customer service reports/market analysis/_____) that our sales team should be aware of?

(5) Salesperson to External Stakeholders or Partners:

1. How can we enhance our partnership by integrating insights from our (customer feedback/marketing analysis/_____)?

2. What opportunities do you see for our collaboration to adapt to the (changing needs of the market/customer expectations/_____)?

3. How can we leverage our (marketing/sales/_____) strategies to support (mutual growth/customer satisfaction/_____)?

4. In what ways can your insights into (market trends/customer behavior/_____) help inform our (product development/sales strategies/_____)?

5. How can we better align our (sales and marketing efforts/strategic goals/_____) with your (expectations/needs/_____) to create a (cohesive strategy/unified approach/_____) for mutual clients?

b. TEAM SELLING APPROACHES:

Team selling is a crucial strategy for handling complex sales and large accounts. These questions are crafted to delve into the essence of collaborative selling, focusing on clear role distribution, leveraging diverse expertise, and fostering internal synergy. They aim to guide you in optimizing your collective approach to achieve a harmonized and impactful client engagement, where every member's contribution is geared towards crafting tailored and compelling solutions for customers.

(1) Salesperson to Client:

1. How can our (team's diverse expertise/client-specific strategies/_____) bring the most value to your business objectives?

2. In what ways can we leverage our (collective knowledge/technical support/_____) to address your specific challenges more effectively?

3. How can our (cross-functional team approach/role-specific contributions/_____) enhance the solution we're proposing for your (needs/goals/_____)?

4. Can you share insights on past experiences where a (multi-disciplinary team/combined expertise/_____) approach from a vendor was beneficial for your projects?

5. How can we improve the aspects of our (team selling approach/role clarity/_____) to better meet your expectations and requirements?

6. How do you perceive the value added by involving specialists from our (product development/customer service/_____) teams in our discussions?

7. What are your thoughts on our proposed (success metrics/incentive structures/_____) to ensure our team's efforts align with your strategic goals?

8. How can we adapt our internal (training/onboarding/_____) processes to better serve your needs?

9. In what ways can we further tailor our (solution development/communication strategies/_____) to address the nuances of your industry sector?

10. How do you envision our (collaborative solution development/feedback mechanisms/_____) impacting your long-term business outcomes?

(2) Client to Salesperson:

1. Can you clarify how each team member's role contributes to understanding and solving our specific challenges (role definition/contribution/_____)?

2. How do you ensure seamless communication and strategy alignment within your team to serve our account (coordination/alignment/_____)?

3. What mechanisms do you have in place to gather and act upon feedback from clients like us (feedback mechanisms/action plans/_____)?

4. How are your team's success metrics aligned with achieving our goals (alignment/measurement/_____)?

5. In what ways do you tailor your team's approach based on the complexity and scope of a client's needs (adaptation/customization/_____)?

6. How do you ensure each team member involved in our project is well-informed about our specific industry and challenges (industry knowledge/specialization/_____)?

7. Can you describe the training process your team undergoes to prepare for complex sales scenarios like ours (training focus/methodology/_____)?

8. How do you decide which team members to engage for a particular account based on its complexity and requirements (team selection/criteria/_____)?

9. How do your team's incentives motivate them to work collaboratively towards our satisfaction by enhancing (incentive structure/collaboration focus/_____)?

10. What strategies do you use to maintain a high level of (interdepartmental cooperation/strategy application/_____) when addressing large accounts or complex sales?

(3) Salesperson to Self:

1. How can I improve my collaboration with (marketing/product development/_____) to enhance our team selling effectiveness?

2. What additional (knowledge/skills/_____) do I need to gain to contribute more effectively to our team's diverse expertise (sales strategies/customer engagement/_____)?

3. How can I better define my role within the team to (avoid overlaps/maximize coverage/_____) of the client's needs (role clarification/task specialization/_____)?

4. In what ways can I contribute to the success metrics and incentive structures that encourage our team's collaboration (performance metrics/team incentives/_____)?

5. How can I continually adapt and refine our team selling approach by leveraging feedback from clients (client insights/strategy adjustments/_____)?

(4) Salesperson to Colleagues/Internal Team:

1. How can we better define and communicate our (individual roles/team dynamics/_____) to ensure a cohesive team approach?

2. What strategies can we implement to ensure our diverse expertise promotes (skill sharing/knowledge exchange/_____) addressing (client needs/solution customization requirements/_____)?

3. How can we improve our internal (meeting/communication/_____) to facilitate seamless (information sharing/team collaboration/_____) among our team?

4. In what ways can we refine our (goal setting/strategy alignment/_____) to align more closely with our shared (team objectives/client expectations/_____) and client expectations?

5. How can we create more effective (feedback collection/process improvement/_____) to share (strategy refinement/actionable insights/_____) across our team?

(5) Salesperson to External Stakeholders or Partners:

1. How can our (partnership synergies/joint strategies/_____) with you enhance (client satisfaction/increased efficiency/_____) to our mutual clients through a (integrated solutions/cohesive experience/_____)?

2. What (market trends/customer feedback/_____) can you advise that might help us better achieve (role clarity/effective delegation/_____) for serving shared clients?

3. In what ways can we align our (performance targets/reward systems/_____) with the goals of our (mutual growth/client success/_____) to encourage (team unity/joint initiatives/_____)?

4. How can we leverage your (industry knowledge/technical skills/_____) to enhance our (skill development/strategy understanding/_____) programs for team members involved in joint (collaborative sales/market penetration/_____) efforts?

5. What (regular check-ins/surveys/_____) can we establish with you to ensure our collaborative (product innovation/service improvement/_____) programs meet client needs effectively?

c. **ADDITIONAL CONSIDERATIONS:**

These questions guide the exploration of team selling and cross-functional collaboration, essential for delivering superior customer experiences. Focusing on fostering a customer-centric approach, leveraging collaborative technologies, enhancing cross-team understanding, and maintaining engagement beyond the sale, they aim to unify efforts across departments. This approach ensures solutions are tailored to customer needs, supporting a strategy that prioritizes long-term partnerships and continuous improvement based on customer feedback.

(1) Salesperson to Client:

1. How can our (team collaboration/customer-centric culture/_____) improve your (experience/satisfaction/_____) with our solutions?

2. In what ways can our (technology tools/communication platforms/_____) enhance our (service delivery/relationship/_____) with you?

3. How do our efforts in (cross-training/post-sale collaboration/_____) align with your expectations for (support/engagement/_____)?

4. What insights can you provide on how our (internal feedback mechanisms/joint strategy sessions/_____) have impacted your (decision-making process/project outcomes/_____)?

5. How does our approach to (customer experience management/technology integration/_____) meet your needs for (transparency/reliability/_____)?

6. How can our collaborative approach to (solution development/customer support/_____) address your (specific needs/challenges/_____) more effectively?

7. In what ways can our use of (CRM systems/mobile sales tools/_____) enhance your (buying experience/product usage/_____) with us?

8. What feedback do you have on how our (internal team collaboration/communication channels/_____) impact your (project success/customer satisfaction/_____)?

9. How do our efforts in (cross-functional team involvement/technology integration/_____) align with your goals for (business growth/operational efficiency/_____)?

10. Can you share how the (personalized solutions/consultative advice/_____) provided by our team has influenced your (decision-making process/strategy development/_____)?

(2) Client to Salesperson:

1. How do your (internal collaborations/technology tools/_____) ensure a consistent and (seamless/effective/_____) customer experience?

2. Can you describe how (cross-functional teams/communication channels/_____) contribute to solving my specific (challenges/needs/_____)?

3. What role does (feedback collection/cross-training/_____) play in enhancing the (solutions/services/_____) you offer to clients like us?

4. How are (joint strategy sessions/technology platforms/_____) used to maintain alignment on our (goals/projects/_____)?

5. In what ways do your (post-sale support/collaborative solution development/_____) practices ensure ongoing (satisfaction/improvement/_____)?

6. How does your organization's customer-centric culture (foster collaboration/ensure customer satisfaction/_____) across departments to enhance our overall experience?

7. In what ways does cross-training among your departments (improve service quality/enhance team empathy/_____) to offer unified solutions to clients like us?

8. How does your team leverage shared access CRM systems (to track customer interactions/to customize solutions/_____) effectively for collaborative selling?

9. Can you provide examples of how cross-functional collaboration (resolved a client issue/enhanced a customer experience/_____) in the past?

10. What steps does your organization take to ensure all team members are aligned on the goals and expectations of our project (through regular updates/joint strategy sessions/_____)?

(3) Salesperson to Self:

1. How can I better integrate (cross-functional insights/customer feedback/_____) into my daily (tasks/strategy/_____)?

2. What steps can I take to enhance my understanding of (technology tools/internal communication channels/_____) for improved collaboration?

3. How can I contribute more effectively to (team selling approaches/cross-departmental strategy/_____) for (client satisfaction/project success/_____)?

4. In what areas do I need to seek (cross-training/feedback/_____) to improve my (performance/collaboration/_____) with internal teams?

5. How can I leverage (CRM systems/project management software/_____) to facilitate better (team coordination/client engagement/_____)?

(4) Salesperson to Colleagues/Internal Team:

1. How can we enhance our (communication channels/strategy alignment/_____) to improve our (team selling effectiveness/customer experience/_____)?

2. In what ways can we better use (technology and tools/feedback mechanisms/_____) to ensure a cohesive approach to (client challenges/solution development/_____)?

3. What best practices should we adopt in (cross-training/joint strategy sessions/_____) to foster a more (collaborative/innovative/_____) team environment?

4. How can we strengthen our (internal collaboration/customer-centric culture/_____) to enhance our collective ability to meet (client needs/market demands/_____)?

5. What actions can we take to ensure that our (role definitions/success metrics and incentives/_____) support (team cohesion/shared objectives/_____)?

(5) Salesperson to External Stakeholders or Partners:

1. How can our partnership leverage (shared technology tools/cross-functional collaboration/_____) to offer (enhanced value/unique solutions/_____) to our customers?

2. In what ways can we collaborate on (training and onboarding/cross-training initiatives/_____) to better understand and address our mutual (client's needs/industry challenges/_____)?

3. How can we establish (communication platforms/joint strategy sessions/_____) that facilitate (seamless information flow/effective cooperation/_____) between our teams?

4. What steps can we take to ensure our (collaboration/technology integration/_____) aligns with our shared goals for (customer satisfaction/innovation/_____)?

5. How can we continuously improve our (services/products/_____) for our customers by utilizing our collective insights from (feedback loops/cross-functional teams/_____)?

18. MINDSET AND ATTITUDE

A.   CULTIVATING POSITIVITY:

Navigating the pressures of sales requires more than just skill; it demands a positive mindset and proactive stress management. These questions are intended to uncover practices that foster positivity, gratitude, and mindfulness in sales environments. By discussing ways to cultivate these attributes, you can enhance personal well-being, foster stronger client relationships, and drive success through a healthier, more resilient approach to your work and interactions.

(1) For Salesperson to Client:

1. How do you maintain a positive outlook when faced with (sales challenges/difficult negotiations/_____)?

2. In what ways do you practice (gratitude/appreciation/_____) within your professional relationships?

3. How has (mindfulness/stress reduction techniques/_____) impacted your approach to sales?

4. Can you share an experience where a (positive mindset/resilient attitude/_____) led to (a successful sale/overcoming objections/_____)?

5. How do you balance the pressures of (sales targets/client expectations/_____) with personal well-being?

6. How do you believe a (positive attitude/empathetic approach/_____) from our sales team impacts your decision-making process?

7. Can you share how (personalized communication/a consultative approach/_____) from us could enhance your experience and trust in our solutions?

8. How do you think we can improve the (service/product presentation/) with a more (customer-centric/positive/) approach?

9. How important is it for you that our team shows (active listening/empathy/_____) during our discussions and sales process?

10. In what ways can we make our meetings more (engaging/productive/_____) for you, focusing on positive outcomes and solutions?

(2) For Client to Salesperson:

1. How do your (positivity practices/gratitude exercises/_____) contribute to your approach in sales?

2. Can you provide examples of how a (positive outlook/optimistic perspective/_____) has helped overcome (client objections/challenging scenarios/_____)?

3. What role does (gratitude/positivity/_____) play in your daily interactions with (clients/colleagues/_____)?

4. How do you ensure a (stress-reduced/positive/_____) environment for both your team and clients?

5. What (mindfulness practices/techniques for stress reduction/_____) do you recommend for managing the fast-paced nature of sales?

6. Can you provide instances where (positive affirmations/visualization techniques/_____) directly contributed to overcoming sales obstacles?

7. How does your team incorporate (gratitude practices/mindfulness/_____) in your daily sales routines, and what impact has it had?

8. What strategies do you use to ensure a (stress-free/constructive/_____) communication flow with clients like us?

9. How do you balance the pressures of achieving sales targets with maintaining a (positive mindset/healthy work-life balance/_____)?

10. What role does (team morale/individual mindset/_____) play in achieving success in complex sales scenarios, and how is it cultivated?

(3) For Salesperson to Self:

1. What daily (affirmations/positive statements/_____) can I use to boost my (positivity/resilience/_____) in sales?

2. How can I incorporate (gratitude/a gratitude journal/_____) into my daily routine to improve my sales mindset?

3. What (mindfulness techniques/stress reduction exercises/_____) can help me manage stress and maintain focus?

4. In what ways can I turn challenging (sales experiences/client interactions/_____) into opportunities for growth?

5. How can I ensure that my approach to sales reflects a balance between (achieving targets/maintaining personal well-being/_____)?

(4) For Salesperson to Colleagues/Internal Team:

1. How can we encourage each other to maintain a positive outlook despite (sales challenges/tough negotiations/_____)?

2. What team practices can we adopt to foster a culture of (gratitude/positivity/_____)?

3. How can we support each other in (stress management/mindfulness practices/_____)?

4. In what ways can we collaborate to turn (sales challenges/learning opportunities/_____) into growth?

5. How can we balance our drive for (sales success/the well-being of our team/_____)?

(5) For Salesperson to External Stakeholders or Partners:

1. How can our partnership reflect a shared commitment to (positivity/well-being/_____)?

2. What practices can we adopt to ensure a positive experience for our (mutual clients/teams/_____)?

3. How can we support each other to incorporate (mindfulness/stress reduction/_____) into our sales strategies?

4. In what ways can we collaborate to foster a culture of (gratitude/positivity/_____) across our teams?

5. How can our partnership help us navigate (sales challenges/with a positive mindset/_____)?

b. **RESILIENCE:**

These questions aim to delve into resilience strategies within the sales process, focusing on overcoming challenges, leveraging failures for growth, and nurturing a supportive environment. By fostering discussions on these topics, you and clients can discover ways to build a resilient mindset essential for thriving in a competitive landscape, ensuring long-term success, and maintaining a positive outlook through ups and downs.

(1) For Salesperson to Client:

1. How can we assist you in developing a resilient mindset to navigate (market fluctuations/challenges/_____) effectively?

2. In what ways can our (support/services/) help you view (setbacks/rejections/_____) as opportunities for growth in your industry?

3. Can we offer (training/sessions/_____) on coping strategies for handling industry-specific (rejections/challenges/_____)?

4. Would you be interested in case studies demonstrating how other clients turned (failures/setbacks/_____) into success stories?

5. How can our (products/services/_____) provide you with the support network needed to overcome (challenges/setbacks/_____)?

6. What type of (feedback/support/_____) mechanisms can we implement to help you leverage (negative feedback/critical insights/_____) for improvement?

7. How can we tailor our (communication/engagement/_____) to reinforce the importance of resilience in achieving long-term (goals/success/_____)?

8. Would you find value in a collaborative review of past (challenges/setbacks/_____) to identify learning (opportunities/strategies/_____) for future resilience?

9. Can we introduce you to our network of (experts/mentors/_____) who can provide guidance and support in your industry's specific challenges?

10. How might we better support your ongoing efforts to build a (strong/resilient/_____) organizational culture in the face of adversity?

(2) For Client to Salesperson:

1. How does your company approach (failure/setbacks/_____) in a way that contributes to (learning/growth/_____)?

2. Can you share examples of how your organization has overcome (significant challenges/failures/_____)?

3. What support systems does your company have in place for clients facing (challenges/setbacks/_____)?

4. How do you ensure your team maintains (resilience/a positive outlook/_____) during (difficult sales cycles/challenging times/_____)?

5. In what ways does your organization foster a culture of (learning from mistakes/failures/_____)?

6. How can your (products/services/_____) assist our company in building a stronger (resilience strategy/support network/_____)?

7. What role do (mentors/support networks/_____) play within your organization in dealing with (challenges/adversity/_____)?

8. Can you provide insights or advice on developing (resilience/adaptive strategies/_____) within our team based on your experiences?

9. How does your team adapt (strategies/approaches/_____) based on (setbacks/feedback/_____) from clients like us?

10. What measures do you take to ensure (continuous improvement/resilience/_____) in your sales approach?

(3) For Salesperson to Self:

1. How can I improve my approach to (failure/setbacks/_____) to view them as opportunities for (learning/growth/_____)?

2. What lessons have I learned from (past challenges/failures/_____) that I can apply to future sales strategies?

3. How can I strengthen my (support network/mentoring relationships/_____) to gain perspective during challenging times?

4. In what ways can I cultivate a mindset that embraces (learning from mistakes/constructive feedback/_____) for personal and professional development?

5. How can I integrate (mindfulness/stress reduction techniques/_____) into my daily routine to manage the pressures of the sales environment more effectively?

(4) For Salesperson to Colleagues/Internal Team:

1. How can we collectively develop strategies to cope with (rejection/setbacks/_____) and view them as opportunities for (growth/learning/_____)?

2. What can we learn from each other's experiences with (failures/challenges/_____) to enhance our team's resilience?

3. In what ways can we strengthen our (support network/team cohesion/_____) to provide encouragement during challenging times?

4. How can we better share and apply lessons learned from (mistakes/feedback/_____) to improve our sales strategies?

5. What practices can we adopt as a team to integrate (mindfulness/stress reduction/_____) techniques, enhancing our collective ability to manage sales pressures?

(5) For Salesperson to External Stakeholders or Partners:

1. How can we collaborate to create a (resilience strategy/support system/_____) that benefits both our teams during challenges?

2. In what ways have you successfully navigated (setbacks/failures/_____) in your organization, and how can those lessons apply to our collaboration?

3. Can you share how your (support networks/mentorship programs/_____) have bolstered resilience among your (team members/senior executives/_____)?

4. What joint initiatives can we undertake to foster a culture of (learning from failure/continuous improvement/_____) across our partnership?

5. How do you envision our collaboration enhancing the (adaptability/resilience/_____) of both our organizations in facing market challenges?

c. **MOTIVATION:**

These questions delve into harnessing motivation in sales, examining how personal and professional incentives can boost performance and engagement. They are designed to uncover how setting personal rewards and visualizing success can directly impact sales effectiveness and client satisfaction. By focusing on motivation, the aim is to reveal strategies that not only drive sales results but also foster a fulfilling and inspiring environment for sales professionals and their clients.

(1) For Salesperson to Client:

1. How do our (solutions/products/_____) align with what motivates you or your company towards achieving your goals?

2. In discussing potential (solutions/outcomes/_____), what achievements would be most rewarding for your team?

3. Can you share how you envision (success/implementation/_____) of our (products/services/_____) impacting your daily operations positively?

4. What (goals/milestones/_____) are you aiming to achieve that our partnership can help facilitate?

5. Are there specific (rewards/benefits/_____) you're looking forward to by achieving your current project goals?

(2) For Client to Salesperson:

1. How does your company identify and align with clients' (motivations/goals/_____) through your (products/services/_____)?

2. Can you provide examples of how your (solutions/services/_____) have motivated other clients towards success?

3. What (rewards/incentives/_____) do you offer to clients who achieve significant milestones with your products?

4. How do you (personalize/adjust/_____) your approach to meet the varying motivational drivers of your clients?

5. In what ways does your team stay motivated to continuously provide (high-quality service/innovative solutions/_____)?

(3) For Salesperson to Self:

1. What personal (motivators/goals/_____) drive me to excel in my sales performance?

2. How can I create a system of (rewards/self-recognition/_____) for meeting my sales targets?

3. In what ways can I use (visualization/affirmation techniques/_____) to enhance my focus and motivation before a sales call?

4. What lessons have I learned from (rejections/setbacks/_____) that have strengthened my resilience and motivation?

5. How do my personal and professional motivations align with the (values/goals/_____) of the organization I represent?

(4) For Salesperson to Colleagues/Internal Team:

1. How can we support each other in identifying and pursuing our (individual/team/_____) motivators within our sales processes?

2. In what ways can we celebrate (milestones/achievements/_____) together to foster a motivated and cohesive team environment?

3. What strategies can we develop for leveraging our (diverse skills/personal motivations/_____) to enhance team performance?

4. How can we use (feedback/peer coaching/_____) sessions to boost each other's (motivation/performance/_____)?

5. Can we set up a system of (team rewards/recognition/_____) that aligns with our collective sales goals and motivators?

(5)   For Salesperson to External Stakeholders or Partners:

1. How can our collaboration inspire motivation and (achievement/growth/_____) for both our teams and our clients?

2. What mutual (goals/objectives/_____) can we set that would motivate and reward both parties?

3. In what ways can we share and implement (motivational strategies/success stories/_____) to foster a culture of excellence and resilience?

4. Can we identify joint (incentives/rewards/_____) that would encourage our teams to achieve and exceed our collaborative goals?

5. How can the (success/motivation/_____) of one partner serve as an inspiration or catalyst for growth for the other?

19. CONTINUOUS LEARNING AND MARKET ADAPTATION

A.   MARKET TRENDS AND ADAPTATION:

To excel in an ever-changing market, these questions guide discussions on adapting sales strategies by staying informed about industry trends and customer behavior. They address leveraging research, engaging in industry events, and utilizing digital tools for insights, focusing on continuous learning and market adaptation to maintain relevance and effectiveness. This approach ensures you are well-equipped to navigate shifts in the market and meet the evolving needs of their clients.

(1) Salesperson to Client:

1. How can we better align our solutions with your growing needs in the (industry/market/_____)?

2. What (trends/technologies/_____) in your industry are you most excited or concerned about?

3. How do you foresee changes in (consumer behavior/market dynamics/_____) affecting your business in the next year?

4. In what ways can we leverage (digital platforms/social media/_____) to enhance our (communication/service/_____) delivery to you?

5. Can you share insights or feedback from your participation in (industry forums/webinars/_____) that could inform our partnership?

6. How do our (products/services/_____) align with your (long-term goals/sustainability efforts/_____)?

7. What kind of (industry reports/market research/_____) would be most beneficial for you, and how can we assist in providing this?

8. How has your approach to evaluating (vendors/partners/_____) developed with recent market trends?

9. What (new challenges/opportunities/_____) has your business faced because of recent changes in the (market/technology/_____)?

10. How can we collaborate to develop a (flexible/adaptable/_____) strategy that accommodates future market shifts?

(2) Client to Salesperson:

1. How do you stay informed about (industry trends/emerging technologies/_____), and how does this influence your (sales/business/_____) approach?

2. Can you provide examples of how you've adapted your (strategy/operations/_____) in response to (market changes/customer feedback/_____)?

3. What resources do you recommend for staying updated on (industry insights/competitive analysis/_____)?

4. How has your company's (product development/marketing strategy/_____) developed in response to recent industry trends?

5. How do you ensure that your sales team is knowledgeable and prepared to discuss (current industry challenges/technological advancements/_____)?

6. What role does (social media/online networking/_____) play in your strategy for understanding and adapting to market trends?

7. How do you leverage (customer feedback/industry forums/_____) to inform your (sales/product development/_____) strategies?

8. In what ways have you seen success through your participation in (trade shows/conferences/_____)?

9. How does your team use (CRM systems/project management software/_____) to collaborate and stay aligned with market changes?

10. What strategies have you implemented to ensure your sales approach remains (flexible/innovative/_____) in the face of industry shifts?

(3) Salesperson to Self:

1. How can I incorporate (continuous learning/market research/_____) into my daily routine to stay ahead in my industry?

2. What (new skills/technologies/_____) do I need to learn to better adapt to the developing market demands?

3. How can I use (feedback loops/social media/_____) to enhance my understanding of (client needs/industry trends/_____)?

4. What steps can I take to ensure I'm leveraging the latest (industry reports/competitive analysis/_____) in my sales strategy?

5. How can I improve my participation in (industry forums/webinars/_____) to gain insights and network with peers?

(4) Salesperson to Colleagues/Internal Team:

1. How can we improve our use of (CRM systems/project management software/_____) to enhance cross-functional collaboration and adapt to market changes?

2. What insights have we gained from recent (industry reports/market research/_____) that could inform our (sales/product development/_____) strategies?

3. How can we better integrate (social media/online platforms/_____) into our strategy to stay connected with industry trends and customer needs?

4. What have we learned from our participation in (trade shows/webinars/_____) that we can apply to our sales approach?

5. How can we encourage more (cross-training/feedback sharing/_____) among our teams to foster a customer-centric culture and adaptability?

(5) Salesperson to External Stakeholders or Partners:

1. How can our partnership better leverage (industry insights/technological advancements/_____) to address future market needs?

2. What role can you play in helping us stay informed about (market trends/consumer behaviors/_____)?

3. How can we collaborate to ensure our (products/services/_____) remain relevant and competitive in a rapidly changing market?

4. What (tools/strategies/_____) do you recommend for improving our (market adaptation/customer engagement/_____) in the upcoming years?

5. How can we work together to incorporate (sustainability/social responsibility/_____) into our sales practices in line with market expectations?

b. **PROFESSIONAL DEVELOPMENT:**

Navigating the dynamic sales landscape demands ongoing professional growth and adaptability to market trends. These questions encourage discussions on enhancing sales competencies and industry insights through targeted training, mentorship, and collaborative learning. They aim to bolster strategies for better serving clients by aligning sales approaches with the latest industry developments, emphasizing the importance of continuous learning in maintaining competitive edge and fostering successful client relationships.

(1) Salesperson to Client:

1. How can we incorporate (ongoing training/professional development/_____) to better meet your unique needs in the (industry/specific market/_____)?

2. What (skills/product knowledge/_____) would you value most from our team to enhance our service to you?

3. In what areas do you see potential for (innovation/improvement/_____) that we can address through further learning or certification?

4. How can mentorship or coaching from our seasoned professionals support your business goals in (specific areas/overall strategy/_____)?

5. Can you share feedback on how cross-functional knowledge sharing within our team could improve our (customer engagement/sales strategy/_____) for you?

6. What insights or updates from (product development/marketing/_____) departments would be most valuable for you?

7. How do you view the role of (professional development programs/structured learning paths/_____) in fostering a long-term partnership between us?

8. What specific (industry trends/technological advancements/_____) should we focus on in our professional development to better serve you?

9. How can we leverage our (internal coaching/mentorship programs/_____) to address your unique challenges and opportunities?

10. What outcomes would you expect from our investment in (continuous learning/market adaptation strategies/_____) in terms of our service delivery to you?

(2) Client to Salesperson:

1. How does your ongoing professional development influence the (quality/innovation/_____) of the solutions you offer?

2. What recent (certifications/courses/_____) have you or your team completed that enhance your understanding of our industry?

3. Can you describe how mentorship within your organization has shaped your approach to (customer service/sales strategy/_____)?

4. How does cross-functional knowledge sharing in your company impact the (solutions/services/_____) you provide to us?

5. What measures do you take to ensure continuous learning and adaptation in response to (market changes/customer feedback/_____)?

6. How do your professional development activities align with the latest (market trends/industry standards/_____) to ensure you're providing the most up-to-date solutions?

7. In what ways have your (training programs/certifications/_____) directly impacted the quality and effectiveness of the solutions you offer to clients like us?

8. Can you share examples of how mentorship or coaching within your organization has directly benefited clients through improved (service quality/solution customization/_____)?

9. How does your team's commitment to continuous (learning/development/) influence your approach to solving unique (challenges/problems/) presented by clients in our (industry/sector/_____)?

10. What strategies do you employ to ensure that all members of your sales team are not just informed about but engaged in ongoing (professional development/training/) to better serve diverse (client needs/market demands/)?

(3) Salesperson to Self:

1. What specific (skills/areas of expertise/_____) do I need to develop to stay ahead in my (industry/sales role/_____)?

2. How can I actively seek (mentorship/coaching/_____) to navigate my career path and improve my sales effectiveness?

3. In what ways can I engage in cross-functional learning to broaden my understanding of (product development/customer service/_____)?

4. What personal rewards system can I set up for achieving my (sales targets/professional development goals/_____)?

5. How can I use visualization techniques to enhance my performance in (sales presentations/client meetings/_____)?

(4) Salesperson to Colleagues/Internal Team:

1. How can we create structured learning paths that benefit our entire team in areas of (sales techniques/industry knowledge/_____)?

2. What insights from (mentorship sessions/knowledge-sharing workshops/_____) can we integrate into our collective sales strategy?

3. How do you suggest we enhance our cross-functional collaboration to leverage (diverse expertise/new technologies/_____) in our sales process?

4. In what ways can our team collectively celebrate successes and learn from (failures/setbacks/_____) to foster a positive and resilient culture?

5. What role can each of us play in contributing to a culture of (continuous learning/adaptability/_____) within our team and organization?

(5) Salesperson to External Stakeholders or Partners:

1. How can our collaboration support your (professional development goals/understanding of market trends/_____)?

2. What opportunities do you see for us to engage in joint (learning initiatives/industry events/_____) that could benefit our partnership?

3. How can we better leverage technology and tools to facilitate (knowledge sharing/cross-training/_____) between our organizations?

4. What feedback do you have on how our team's (professional growth/certification efforts/_____) have affected our service to you?

5. In what ways can we align our (professional development strategies/learning paths/_____) to better meet the needs of your business and industry?

c. **ADDITIONAL CONSIDERATIONS:**

In a rapidly changing market, staying ahead requires a proactive approach to learning and adaptation. These questions are crafted to delve into strategies for maintaining relevance through adaptability skills training, innovation workshops, and feedback loops for continuous improvement. They aim to enhance personal and professional growth, ensuring you and your strategies remain aligned with evolving market demands and client needs, fostering a dynamic and responsive sales environment.

(1) Salesperson to Client:

1. How can we tailor our approach to align with your evolving needs and (market trends/technology shifts/_____)?

2. In what ways can our (product/service/solution) adapt to your future growth and (industry changes/competitive landscape/_____)?

3. What feedback mechanisms can we establish to ensure our solutions continue to meet your (expectations/objectives/_____)?

4. How do you see innovation playing a role in solving your current and (future challenges/operational needs/_____)?

5. How can our team assist in integrating new (strategies/technologies/_____) into your current processes?

6. Can you share how changes in your industry are affecting your (strategy/planning/_____)?

7. What type of (training/support/_____) would make adopting new solutions easier for your team?

8. In what ways can we improve our feedback loop to better understand your (challenges/expectations/_____)?

9. How do you envision our partnership strengthening with the rapid changes in (market trends/technology/_____)?

10. What insights from our (research/innovation efforts/_____) have you found most valuable in planning your strategy?

(2) Client to Salesperson:

1. How does your company stay ahead of (market trends/technological advancements/_____) to ensure the solutions you offer remain relevant?

2. Can you provide examples of how you've adapted your offerings in response to (industry changes/customer feedback/_____)?

3. What processes do you have in place for gathering and implementing customer (feedback/insights/_____)?

4. How often do you (update/train/_____) your team on new market trends and technologies?

5. How do you ensure your (products/services/_____) evolve with your customers' growing needs?

6. In what ways can you show the adaptability of your (solutions/strategy/_____) to our specific industry challenges?

7. What kind of support and (training/resources/_____) do you offer to clients undergoing transitions?

8. How do your innovation and creativity workshops contribute to (solving client problems/developing new solutions/_____)?

9. Can you share a success story where feedback led to significant (improvement/innovation/_____) in your offering?

10. How does your company facilitate cross-functional knowledge sharing to benefit your (clients/strategies/_____)?

(3) Salesperson to Self:

1. How can I better incorporate customer feedback into my (sales approach/strategy development/_____)?

2. In what areas do I need further (training/development/_____) to stay ahead of industry changes?

3. What new (skills/technologies/_____) should I learn to improve my adaptability in sales?

4. How can I foster a more (innovative/creative/_____) approach to problem-solving in my sales process?

5. How can I improve my resilience to navigate through (market changes/rejections/_____) more effectively?

(4) Salesperson to Colleagues/Internal Team:

1. How can we collaborate more effectively to integrate (market insights/customer feedback/_____) into our sales strategy?

2. What (training/workshops/_____) would benefit our team to enhance our collective adaptability skills?

3. How can we better share (knowledge/insights/_____) across departments to improve our sales approach?

4. In what ways can we create more effective feedback loops to drive continuous (improvement/innovation/_____)?

5. How can we support each other in developing personalized learning and development plans that align with our (goals/career paths/_____)?

(5) Salesperson to External Stakeholders or Partners:

1. How can our collaboration facilitate the integration of (new technologies/market trends/_____) into our offerings?

2. In what ways can you contribute to our team's (learning/development/_____) in the context of market adaptation?

3. Can you provide insights or (research/analyses/_____) that can help us better understand our target market's evolving needs?

4. How can we leverage our partnership to foster a culture of (innovation/continuous improvement/_____)?

5. What joint (workshops/training sessions/_____) can we organize to enhance our teams' adaptability and creative problem-solving skills?

20. MEASURING SUCCESS AND ANALYZING PERFORMANCE

A.   SALES ANALYTICS AND KPI TRACKING:

Effective sales analytics and KPI tracking are pivotal for enhancing sales performance and strategic alignment with business goals. This set of questions aims to facilitate discussions on the best practices for utilizing data analytics, defining relevant KPIs, and ensuring continuous improvement through regular analysis. These insights will help tailor sales strategies, achieve targeted outcomes, and maintain competitive edge, benefiting you and your clients alike.

(1) Salesperson to Client:

1. How does our performance measure up against your expectations in terms of (delivery timelines/product quality/_____)?

2. In what ways can we improve our (communication/service delivery/_____) to better meet your KPIs?

3. Can you provide feedback on how effectively our solutions have contributed to your (sales targets/business growth/_____)?

4. What additional metrics would you suggest we track to better align with your business (objectives/strategies/_____)?

5. How can we modify our reporting to give you more insights into (market trends/customer behavior/_____)?

6. What specific outcomes would you like to see from our partnership that would positively impact your (business growth/operational efficiency/_____)?

7. How can we tailor our reporting to provide you with actionable insights into (customer trends/sales performance/_____)?

8. Can we explore any additional metrics that matter most to your strategic (planning/decision-making/_____) process?

9. Would you find value in a more in-depth analysis of how our services impact your (market share/customer acquisition/_____)?

10. How can we better align our KPIs to support your long-term business (objectives/visions/_____)?

(2) Client to Salesperson:

1. How do you measure the success of your solutions in terms of (customer satisfaction/ROI/_____)?

2. Can you share any success stories where your service significantly impacted a client's (sales figures/operational efficiency/_____)?

3. What KPIs do you prioritize in evaluating your performance and making (strategic adjustments/service improvements/_____)?

4. How often do you review and adjust your (sales/growth/_____) strategies based on (market feedback/performance analytics/_____)?

5. How transparent are you in sharing performance (metrics/outcomes/_____) with your clients?

6. How do you ensure the data you track and report is accurately reflecting the current market (conditions/trends/_____)?

7. Can you demonstrate how your (service/product/_____) has directly influenced similar clients' (sales targets/brand recognition/_____)?

8. What processes do you have in place to adjust your KPIs in response to (market shifts/client feedback/_____)?

9. How do you prioritize which KPIs to focus on when formulating your sales strategies and (tactics/goals/_____)?

10. Can you provide examples of how you've used KPI tracking to pivot or change strategy for better client outcomes in the past?

(3) Salesperson to Self:

1. What personal KPIs should I set to track my progress in (customer engagement/sales conversions/_____)?

2. How can I better use data analytics to identify areas for improvement in my (sales techniques/client interactions/_____)?

3. What benchmarks should I set for myself to ensure I'm aligned with the overall business (goals/objectives/_____)?

4. How frequently should I review my sales performance to make timely adjustments to my (approach/strategy/_____)?

5. In what ways can I leverage feedback for continuous personal and professional (development/growth/_____)?

(4) Salesperson to Colleagues/Internal Team:

1. How can we better collaborate to define and track KPIs that reflect our collective contribution to (sales goals/company objectives/_____)?

2. What internal benchmarks should we set to evaluate our team's performance in (cross-selling/upselling/customer retention/_____)?

3. In what ways can regular reporting and analysis improve our (team dynamics/strategy adjustments/_____)?

4. How can we ensure that our sales strategies are flexible enough to adapt to (changing market conditions/customer feedback/_____)?

5. What role can each department play in (contributing to/improving upon/_____) our key sales performance indicators?

(5) Salesperson to External Stakeholders or Partners:

1. How can our partnership influence the KPIs we track to ensure alignment with market (trends/needs/_____)?

2. What insights can you provide that might help us refine our sales strategies and improve our performance metrics?

3. How frequently should we engage in joint reviews of performance data to align on (goals/strategies/_____)?

4. In what ways can your expertise contribute to setting more (relevant/challenging/_____) benchmarks for our sales team?

5. Can you share examples of how collaboration has led to improved (KPI tracking/success measurement/_____) in other partnerships?

b. FEEDBACK LOOPS AND LEARNING FROM LOSSES:

Cultivating a feedback-driven culture is essential for continuous improvement in sales strategies. This set of questions is designed to help you engage with clients and internal teams to extract valuable insights from both wins and losses. By embracing structured debriefs, reinforcing the sharing of lessons learned from setbacks, and conducting thorough customer satisfaction surveys, you can pinpoint areas for enhancement, adapt your approach, and foster growth, all while staying aligned with evolving market demands and customer expectations.

(1) Salesperson to Client:

1. How can we improve our approach to (meeting your needs/solving your challenges/_____) based on your experience with us?

2. In reflecting on our discussions, what could have been done differently to (align with your expectations/provide a better solution/_____)?

3. Can you share insights on how our (product/service/_____) compares with your chosen solution in terms of (value/efficiency/_____)?

4. Would you be open to discussing the (specific features/offer terms/_____) that led to your decision not to proceed with us?

5. After our last conversation, what feedback can you provide that could help us enhance our (customer engagement/sales process/_____)?

6. What key factor(s) influenced your decision to go with another provider, and how can we address these areas (product features/service delivery/_____) for future consideration?

7. Could you provide specific feedback on how our (communication/solution presentation/_____) could be improved to better meet your expectations?

8. In your view, what strengths did our competitor exhibit that swayed your decision, and how might we (adapt/enhance/_____) our offering in response?

9. How would you rate the importance of (cost/value-added services/_____) in your decision-making process, and where did our proposal fall short?

10. Looking forward, what changes or enhancements in our (products/services/_____) would make you reconsider our solution for your needs?

(2) Client to Salesperson:

1. How does your company process feedback from lost sales to improve (product offerings/customer experience/_____)?

2. Can you explain how past losses have influenced changes in your (sales approach/product development/_____)?

3. What measures do you take to ensure customer feedback leads to actionable improvements in your (sales tactics/offerings/_____)?

4. How frequently does your team review and adapt its strategies based on customer feedback and (market trends/competitive analysis/_____)?

5. In what ways do you believe your service could be enhanced based on feedback from customers like myself?

6. Can you detail the specific criteria you use to evaluate feedback from clients, especially those that choose not to proceed with your solution?

7. How does your company ensure that lessons learned from lost sales are effectively (communicated/implemented/_____) across the (sales team/organization/_____)?

8. What (initiatives/changes/_____) have been put in place because of learning from past sales losses, and how have they impacted your sales strategy?

9. In terms of customer feedback, what (channels/methods/_____) have proven most effective for your team in gathering actionable insights?

10. How do you handle feedback from lost sales, and what approach do you find most (effective/inspiring/_____) for turning these experiences into opportunities for growth?

(3) Salesperson to Self:

1. What can I learn from this lost sale to better identify and meet the needs of future (clients/prospects/_____)?

2. How can I adjust my (pitch/strategy/_____) to better address the (concerns/preferences/_____) of my target audience?

3. What feedback have I received that indicates a need for improvement in my (product knowledge/communication skills/_____)?

4. How can I use the experience of lost sales to strengthen my (resilience/adaptability/_____) in future sales scenarios?

5. In what ways can I enhance my approach to (gathering/using/_____) feedback to prevent similar losses in the future?

(4) Salesperson to Colleagues/Internal Team:

1. How can we collectively improve our approach to learning from lost sales to enhance our (team performance/customer engagement/_____)?

2. What insights have you gained from customer feedback that can help us refine our (sales tactics/offerings/_____)?

3. In our next team meeting, can we discuss strategies for better capturing and acting on feedback from (lost opportunities/current clients/_____)?

4. How can our team more effectively share and implement learnings from lost sales across different (departments/teams/_____)?

5. Can we establish a more structured process for debriefing on lost sales and integrating those learnings into our (sales strategies/training programs/_____)?

(5) Salesperson to External Stakeholders or Partners:

1. Based on your observations, how can we better use feedback from the market to improve our (product offerings/sales approach/_____)?

2. From your perspective, what are the most common reasons our mutual clients choose alternative solutions, and how can we address these issues?

3. Can you share examples of how feedback from lost sales has been successfully integrated into (product development/marketing strategies/_____)?

4. How can we collaborate more effectively to ensure feedback from all stakeholders is considered in our (continuous improvement/service development/_____) processes?

5. What role do you see external partners playing in helping us (analyze/learn/_____) from lost sales to enhance our market position?

c. **ADDITIONAL CONSIDERATIONS:**

Navigating the complexities of sales demands a keen focus on performance analysis and adaptability. These questions are crafted for discussions with clients, self-evaluation, team collaboration, and partnership dialogues. They aim to uncover opportunities for refining sales strategies, improving client interactions, and fostering a culture of continuous learning. Engage with these queries to drive actionable insights, enhance service quality, and ensure alignment with evolving market demands and individual growth goals.

(1) Salesperson to Client:

1. How can we improve our service to better meet your (expectations/needs/_____) based on your recent experience with us?

2. In reflecting on our ongoing relationship, what areas do you think we could (enhance/optimize/_____) to serve you better?

3. Can you share insights on how our technology and tools facilitated (your decision-making/our collaboration/_____)?

4. What specific aspects of our (product/service/_____) have you found most beneficial, and how can we build on these successes?

5. How effectively do you feel our (incentive/recognition/_____) programs reflect your (values/needs/_____) as a client?

6. How can our implementation of new (technologies/tools/_____) make your experience with us more (efficient/effective/_____)?

7. Given our goal for continuous improvement, what feedback mechanism would you prefer to keep us informed about your (satisfaction/requirements/_____)?

8. In terms of adaptability, how can we better respond to your (needs/preferences/_____) in real-time?

9. Regarding our sales approach, what additional (services/support/_____) would create more value for your business?

10. To ensure we are aligning with your business objectives, how often would you like to review and possibly reset our (goals/strategies/_____) together?

(2) Client to Salesperson:

1. How do you (track/measure/_____) success in your interactions with clients like me?

2. Can you explain how feedback from clients is incorporated into your (sales strategy/training programs/_____)?

3. How does your team use technology to ensure you're meeting (my/our industry's/_____) specific needs?

4. What role does peer review play in your approach to (client engagement/sales strategy/_____)?

5. In what ways do you believe continuous learning and development have impacted your ability to serve your clients?

6. Can you share examples of how you have adapted your sales strategy in response to (customer feedback/market changes/_____)?

7. How do you ensure that your sales team stays informed and knowledgeable about (our industry/your product offerings/_____)?

8. In what ways do you gather and use customer feedback to improve your (products/services/_____)?

9. How are successes and failures discussed within your team, and how does this influence your approach to (customer service/sales tactics/_____)?

10. What specific training or development programs have you found most impactful in enhancing your ability to meet (client needs/sales targets/_____)?

(3) Salesperson to Self:

1. How can I better use sales performance tools to monitor my (progress/goals/_____) more effectively?

2. What specific areas of feedback should I seek from peers and clients to enhance my (skills/strategies/_____)?

3. How do my personal reward systems align with my long-term career (goals/aspirations/_____) in sales?

4. In what ways can I incorporate continuous learning into my daily routine to stay ahead in (my industry/technology trends/_____)?

5. Reflecting on my performance, what innovative (approaches/knowledge/_____) can I adopt to improve my sales outcomes?

(4) Salesperson to Colleagues/Internal Team:

1. How can we foster a more collaborative environment to share our (successes/failures/_____) for mutual learning?

2. What (technology/tools/_____) have you found most effective for (tracking performance/learning new skills/_____)?

3. How can we better align our incentive structures to motivate our team towards (collective goals/continuous improvement/_____)?

4. Can we set up a regular schedule for cross-functional knowledge-sharing sessions to improve our (sales strategies/customer engagement/_____)?

5. What feedback mechanisms can we implement to ensure ongoing (communication/collaboration/_____) across departments?

(5) Salesperson to External Stakeholders or Partners:

1. How can our collaboration with you provide insights into (market trends/customer preferences/_____) that could inform our sales strategies?

2. In what ways can technology enhance our partnership to create more value for (our customers/both parties/_____)?

3. What learning opportunities can we explore together to stay ahead of (industry changes/competitive pressures/_____)?

4. How can we continuously improve our (products/services/_____) by leveraging feedback from our joint ventures?

5. What incentive programs could we co-develop to recognize and motivate the sales teams across our (partnership/industry/_____)?

HELP OTHERS EXCEL IN SALES

I'm adding this section again so you don't please forget to help.

Your feedback and experience are valuable, especially to those looking to improve their sales skills. There are many sales professionals and individuals with sales duties searching for ways to enhance their performance. Your review could provide the guidance they need.

Think of your review not just as feedback, but as a recommendation and a sign of the book's value. If "2100 Sales Questions for Peak Performance" has given you useful insights or strategies, sharing your thoughts in a review could:

- Point others towards effective sales strategies and skills.
- Help someone improve their ability to mentor, lead, and close deals.
- Offer a new perspective or strategy that could be crucial for someone else.
- Encourage positive changes in someone's sales approach or career.

By leaving a review, you're helping to expand the knowledge and skills of the sales community. If you found this book beneficial, consider letting others know. The best tools are often those recommended by peers.

If you enjoyed the book, please leave a review where you bought it. Your input is very important.

To leave your review, please scan this QR code:

Thanks for your support and for promoting excellence in sales.

Best,

Mauricio

Appendix No 1

Questions for Trade shows and Networking Events

Questions tailored for engaging potential clients at trade shows and networking events, where the dynamic is a mix of casual and professional, and the goal is to make a memorable impression while gathering leads.

1. What's been the highlight of the (trade show/networking event/_____) for you so far?

2. How does this event align with your current projects in (your industry/your field/_____)?

3. I'm curious, what trends in (your industry/your field/_____) are you finding most intriguing lately?

4. Have you come across any challenges recently where you're seeking (innovative solutions/new technologies/_____)?

5. When exploring new (products/services/_____), what features catch your eye (features/advantages/_____)?

6. Could I share insights on (emerging technologies/industry innovations/_____) that might interest you?

7. What criteria do you consider most critical when exploring (new industry solutions/partnerships/_____)?

8. What's motivating you to attend this (trade show/exhibition/_____)?

9. Is there a specific (problem/goal/challenge) that's top of mind for you in (your industry/your field/_____) this year?

10. In comparing (solutions/vendors/_____) in our industry, what factors do you prioritize for your needs (factors/priorities/_____)?

11. Reflecting on past experiences, what's one thing you wish (product/service/_____) providers understood better?

12. Are there aspects of your (operations/business strategy/_____) where you're exploring significant (improvements/changes/_____)?

13. Would it be helpful to discuss some (industry case studies/success stories/_____) that might relate to your current interests?

14. What's your vision for (integrating new technologies/implementing strategic changes/_____) in the coming year?

15. Transitioning to new (solutions/technologies/_____) can be complex; what concerns do you usually encounter (concerns/challenges/_____)?

16. Beyond this event, what's the best way for you to receive (updates/insights/_____) that could benefit your projects?

17. Would a (less formal follow-up/meeting/_____) to explore potential synergies be something you're open to (follow-up/synergies/_____)?

18. If there were one (problem/need/_____) you could address with a magic wand, what would it be?

19. Would joining our (community newsletter/industry insights series/_____) for (industry insights/latest trends/_____) be of interest to you?

20. How can we facilitate a (connection/follow-up/_____) that respects your (pace/preferences/_____) following the trade show?

Appendix No 2

Questions for Cold Calling

Strategic set of questions tailored for cold calling prospects. Designed to open dialogues and foster interest, these questions serve as a foundation for meaningful conversations, helping you to engage prospects effectively and set the stage for future discussions about potential partnerships or sales opportunities.

1. Could you share what your main (focus/priority/_____) is right now in your (business/role/_____)?

2. I'm curious, how are you currently addressing (industry challenges/specific needs/_____) in your organization?

3. What (strategies/solutions/_____) have you explored to improve your (sales efficiency/customer engagement/_____)?

4. In your experience, what has been the most effective way to (reduce costs/increase efficiency/_____) in your operations?

5. What would you say are the top (goals/objectives/_____) for your team this quarter?

6. How are you adapting to the latest (industry trends/technological advancements/_____) in your sector?

7. Can I share how we've helped others in your industry overcome similar (challenges/obstacles/_____)?

8. What's your take on the current (market trends/competitive landscape/_____) affecting your business?

9. Do you see value in exploring new (technologies/methodologies/_____) to achieve your current goals?

10. How important is it for you to find solutions that offer (scalability/cost-effectiveness/_____)?

11. Could we schedule a brief meeting to discuss innovative strategies for enhancing your (customer experience/operational efficiency/_____)?

12. What challenges have you faced in finding the right (partners/solutions/_____) in the past?

13. How do you prioritize (investment decisions/technology adoption/_____) within your current strategy?

14. Are there any upcoming projects where you're exploring (new partnerships/technology implementations/_____)?

15. What factors do you consider when evaluating new (vendors/solutions/_____) for your business?

16. Would you be open to a conversation about potential ways to (optimize your workflow/increase your market share/_____)?

17. How do you foresee your (business model/customer engagement strategies/_____) evolving in the next year?

18. What's been your biggest (hindrance/setback/_____) in achieving your recent goals?

19. Would you find a (demo/consultation/_____) useful in understanding how our solutions could meet your needs?

20. How can we help support your vision for (growth/innovation/_____) in the coming months?

Appendix No 3

Follow-up Questions

Follow-up questions are crucial for deepening engagement and understanding in sales conversations. They're designed to clarify responses and demonstrate your genuine interest in meeting your prospect or client's needs, applicable across a wide range of scenarios.

1. Can you expand on what you mentioned about (your current situation/our discussion/_____)?

2. What specific aspects of (our conversation/your requirements/_____) would you like more information on?

3. Could you clarify what you mean by (the term you used/your earlier comment/_____)?

4. How does (the topic we discussed/our proposed solution/_____) align with your (objectives/strategy/_____)?

5. Can you provide an example of how (a related scenario/our suggestion/_____) impacted your (business/decision-making process/_____)?

6. In what ways do you envision (our proposal/your strategy/_____) addressing your (needs/challenges/_____)?

7. What are your key criteria for (making a decision/evaluating options/_____) in this context?

8. How urgent is the need to address (the issue you mentioned/your current challenge/_____)?

9. Are there any other (stakeholders/considerations/_____) that need to be involved in this decision?

10. What additional information can we provide to assist you in (making a decision/understanding our proposal/_____)?

11. Can you tell me more about your (decision-making process/evaluation criteria/_____) for (this type of solution/engaging with new vendors/_____)?

12. What has been your experience with (similar situations/past solutions/_____)?

13. How do you measure success for (an initiative like this/a solution like ours/_____)?

14. What concerns do you have about (adopting a new solution/moving forward with our proposal/_____)?

15. Could you share more about your (timeline/priorities/_____) for (implementing a solution/making a decision/_____)?

16. What would be the ideal outcome for you from (using our product or service/our collaboration/_____)?

17. Are there any (budgetary constraints/financial considerations/_____) we should be aware of?

18. What other (options/solutions/_____) are you currently considering?

19. How do you see (our proposal/this solution/_____) fitting into your overall (plans/operations/_____)?

20. After our conversation, what are the next steps you foresee for (evaluating our proposal/moving forward/_____)?

Appendix No 4

Unlock Your Sales Potential

As a valued reader of "2100 Sales Questions for Peak Performance" we are pleased to offer you exclusive access to a downloadable Excel sheet containing all the questions featured in this book.

This resource helps you navigate through the questions easily and apply them to your sales strategies more effectively.

You can have access to your questions wherever you are and whenever you need them.

Access the Excel sheet by scanning this QR code: